I0761800

The Turks and the Caliphal Army

Letter from the General Editor

The Library of Arabic Literature makes available Arabic editions and English translations of significant works of Arabic literature, with an emphasis on the seventh to nineteenth centuries. The Library of Arabic Literature thus includes texts from the pre-Islamic era to the cusp of the modern period, and encompasses a wide range of genres, including poetry, poetics, fiction, religion, philosophy, law, science, travel writing, history, and historiography.

Books in the series are edited and translated by internationally recognized scholars. They are published as hardcovers in parallel-text format with Arabic and English on facing pages, as English-only paperbacks, and as downloadable Arabic editions. For some texts, the series also publishes separate scholarly editions with full critical apparatus.

The Library encourages scholars to produce authoritative Arabic editions, accompanied by modern, lucid English translations, with the ultimate goal of introducing Arabic's rich literary heritage to a general audience of readers as well as to scholars and students.

The publications of the Library of Arabic Literature are generously supported by Tamkeen under the NYU Abu Dhabi Research Institute Award G1003 and are published by NYU Press.

Philip F. Kennedy
General Editor, Library of Arabic Literature

الرسالة إلى الفتح بن خاقان في مناقب الترك وعامّة جند الخلافة

أبو عثمان الجاحظ

The Turks and the Caliphal Army

AL-JĀḤIẒ

Edited and translated by
Robert G. Hoyland

Volume editor
Bilal Orfali

NEW YORK UNIVERSITY PRESS
New York

NEW YORK UNIVERSITY PRESS
New York

Library of Congress Cataloging-in-Publication Control Number: 2024054777

Please contact the Library of Congress for Cataloging-in-Publication data.

ISBN: 9781479840625 (hardback)
ISBN: 9781479840649 (library ebook)
ISBN: 9781479840632 (consumer ebook)

This book is printed on acid-free paper, and its binding materials are chosen for strength and durability. We strive to use environmentally responsible suppliers and materials to the greatest extent possible in publishing our books.

The manufacturer's authorized representative in the EU for product safety is Mare Nostrum Group B.V., Mauritskade 21D, 1091 GC Amsterdam, The Netherlands. Email: gpsr@mare-nostrum.co.uk.

Series design by Titus Nemeth and Stuart Brown.

Typeset in Sakkal Kitab Medium.

Typesetting and digitization by Stuart Brown.

Manufactured in the United States of America
c10 9 8 7 6 5 4 3 2 1

Table of Contents

Freddie Beeston
In fond memory

Acknowledgments

This book had its beginnings in the academic year of 1994–95 at St. John's College, Oxford. I was in my first year of a Junior Research Fellowship, and Freddie Beeston, the former Laudian Professor of Arabic, had moved back into his old college while he was having medical treatment at the nearby Radcliffe Infirmary. By chance, we were assigned accommodation right next to each other, in the newly opened Garden Quadrangle. This gave us ample opportunity to meet and discuss our mutual passion for Arabic, and both of us went frequently to dinner in Hall, where we could explore our shared interests over a good meal and fine wine. At the time, Freddie was thinking of producing a new translation of al-Jāḥiẓ's epistle on *The Turks*, but he was not satisfied with the published Arabic editions and wished to produce his own. However, his eyesight was not good, and so he asked if I would help him review the manuscripts. This was not the simple task it is today, flitting through beautiful high-resolution images on a sophisticated computer; in the case of the London manuscript of the epistle, for example, we were using slides (which I still have), and it took me a lot of time and effort to transcribe the text. Our progress was slow, for Freddie followed the old-school method of reading Arabic texts, contemplating each word in turn and giving it due consideration, then examining the whole sentence or paragraph to reflect on the ways in which it was more than the sum of its parts. The time flew by, though, in part because it was a joy to spend time with Freddie—he imparted his rich store of knowledge with sprightly ease and was always ready with a joke or an anecdote to illustrate his ideas. Very often, a fortifying drink would be acquired that would further lubricate our brain cells, and college dinners could stretch into the early morning as we deliberated on al-Jāḥiẓ's aims and intentions, digressions and ramblings. By the end of the summer of 1995, however, we had drafted a working edition and made a good start on the translation. Sadly, though, Freddie passed away in September 1995, and I had to decide what to do with the stack of notes and store of memories I had accumulated in my year with Freddie.

Initially, I thought to persuade a publisher with a series on world classics, such as Penguin or Oxford University Press, to include translations of Arabic texts, since at that time only the Qur'an and *The Thousand and One Nights* made the cut. However, it was before 9/11/2001 and no one thought classical Arabic literature would ever be much of a sell. I therefore put the text aside for a time and soon became caught up with other projects and with teaching in my new job at the University of St. Andrews. Yet I did not forget my commitment to see through the *Turks* project Freddie had entrusted to me, and an invitation to attend a planning meeting for the nascent Library of Arabic Literature (LAL) in Abu Dhabi in 2010 gave me a route to achieve that goal. It was given further impetus when my new home institution, the Institute for the Study of the Ancient World at New York University, kindly allowed me to spend a semester at New York University's Abu Dhabi campus in the fall of 2017. During this time, I was able to renew my friendship with Philip Kennedy, whom I had known at Oxford while a PhD student and who actively encouraged me to offer *The Turks* for inclusion in LAL. My many conversations with Phil were as wandering as a Jaḥiẓian divagation, but they were usually insightful, and I learned much from his take on reading and translating Arabic literature.

The process of publishing with LAL entails submitting one's text to a number of eminent scholars for review at several stages. This is both a humbling and a helpful experience, and I am grateful to the two preliminary reviewers, the project editor, and the final reviewer for the rich and constructive feedback they have provided, as well as for their encouragement, which has motivated me to stay the course. I am also grateful to Geert Jan van Gelder, who gave sage advice on how best to produce a single edition from two divergent versions, and to Chip Rossetti, who has always been there in the background, offering his encouragement and gently reminding me of requirements and deadlines.

I owe a more indirect debt to Patricia Crone. She taught me Islamic history when I was an impressionable undergraduate and an idealistic postgraduate. She was such an inspiring and enthusiastic presence in my formative years as a scholar that whenever I engage in any new research, I hear her voice, whether setting out her own views or critiquing mine. I took a special subject with her on resistance to early Abbasid rule, which related to the book she was then writing on the nativist prophets of Iran, and my Introduction below certainly contains echoes and recollections of her thoughts on this fascinating period of history.

But it is to Freddie that I am most beholden. This book begins and ends with him, and in so many ways it is his. I thought about putting his name as coauthor next to mine, or even as sole author, but he cannot give his consent, and I fear it would diminish his name, for I do not come close to him in terms of philological expertise and intimate acquaintance with classical Arabic literature. But I am emboldened by the fact that Freddie was a warm and generous soul, and I think he would have been pleased to see that what he started has finally come to fruition and been made available to all, even if not in the form he originally intended or in the way he would have done it.

Introduction

The Author and His Addressees[1]

Abū ʿUthmān ʿAmr ibn Baḥr al-Kinānī al-Fuqaymī was a famous Muslim prose writer. We know little about his early life, since he came from a relatively humble background, and it was only once he had made a name for himself that he attracted the attention of the scholarly community. He was born in Basra around the year 160/776 and remained there until his adulthood. Later biographers tend to focus on his ugliness, which stemmed from an eye defect that earned him the nickname of al-Jāḥiẓ ("the goggle-eyed"), and on his thirst for knowledge, which saw him as a boy spending much time at the local mosque listening to the orations of preachers and scholars. As a young man, he traveled to Baghdad, which became his second home after his native Basra, and for a short time he worked as a scribe. However, it seems that quite early on, his talents as a creative writer were recognized, and he was able to earn his living by composing essays on topics both serious and humorous for wealthy patrons. A treatise on the imamate that he penned around the year 200/815 won the admiration of the Caliph al-Ma'mūn (r. 198–218/813–33), and from then on, until his death in 255/868 or 869, he wrote for some of the most powerful and influential public figures of his day. The range of his output was vast, covering social, theological, and political subjects and amounting to some two hundred works, of which at least seventy survive wholly or in part.

The two patrons mentioned in al-Jāḥiẓ's treatise *The Turks and the Caliphal Army* are al-Muʿtaṣim, who he says made the initial request to him for an excursus on the Turks, and al-Fatḥ ibn Khāqān, for whom al-Jāḥiẓ reworked and expanded the earlier text.[2] The former was a younger brother of al-Ma'mūn and succeeded him as caliph (r. 218–27/833–42). The latter was a descendant of the Turkic rulers of Farghānah in modern eastern Uzbekistan, whose father had converted to Islam and became one of the first commanders of al-Muʿtaṣim's Turkish guard. He was educated together with al-Muʿtaṣim's son Jaʿfar, and when the latter became caliph in 232/847, taking the regnal name al-Mutawakkil, he appointed al-Fatḥ to high office and sent him on many sensitive diplomatic missions. As well as being a key advisor to the caliph and a favorite at his court, al-Fatḥ offered patronage and support to many literary and scholarly authors, among them al-Jāḥiẓ. He was killed alongside al-Mutawakkil during a palace coup in 247/861.

Cultural Context[3]

The intellectual culture of Iraq during al-Jāḥiz's lifetime was vibrant and diverse. The first Islamic dynasty, the Umayyads (41–132/661–750), had adopted as their capital Damascus, which was a small provincial city relatively remote from the major intellectual centers of the day. However, the Abbasid dynasty, which overthrew the Umayyads in a revolution in 132/750, decided to make Iraq the seat of their rule and built near the old Persian city of Ctesiphon a new capital, Baghdad. It quickly became a wealthy and bustling metropolis, drawing talent from the large, well-educated Christian, Jewish, and Zoroastrian communities of southern Iraq and from farther afield, as the Islamic Empire became more expansive and cosmopolitan. Trade along the Indian Ocean between Baghdad and Chang'an, the capital of China's Tang dynasty, boomed and brought riches to the many port cities along the way, including Basra.

The early Abbasid caliphs, in emulation of their Persian imperial predecessors, began to promote the translation of scientific and literary texts from Greek, Syriac, Persian, and Sanskrit. This snowballed into a full-scale movement as many members of the Iraqi elite joined in and commissioned their own translations. This movement was facilitated by two factors. The first was the spread of paper from around the year 800, which was much cheaper and easier to produce than parchment or papyrus, and this in turn meant that books were more accessible. The well-to-do with intellectual ambitions could go to bookshops or have texts copied, and in this way they could build up their own libraries. The second factor was the increased use of Arabic, which was fast becoming an international language of scholarship.

Al-Jāḥiẓ benefited from this intellectually flourishing scene. He had renowned teachers, such as the theologian Ibrāhīm al-Naẓẓām (d. ca. 225/840) and the philologists Abū ʿUbaydah Maʿmar (d. 209/825) and al-Aṣmaʿī (d. 213/828). He had illustrious contemporaries, like Ḥunayn ibn Isḥāq (d. 260/873), who translated scores of Greek and Syriac texts into Arabic, including a large proportion of the Galenic corpus, and Abū Yūsuf al-Kindī (d. ca. 256/870), who engaged with this stream of scientific data from the ancient world and refashioned it for a Muslim intellectual elite. Furthermore, al-Jāḥiẓ had wealthy and powerful patrons, such as the Caliph al-Muʿtaṣim, the merchant and vizier Ibn al-Zayyāt (d. 233/847), and the chief judge Ibn Abī Du'ād (d. 240/854). This influential and varied patronage meant that al-Jāḥiẓ had access to ample resources and was very well informed about politics and scholarship.

He also had sufficient friends and admirers and was politically savvy enough to survive the turbulence of the court. Many senior figures were ruthlessly ousted in the shift from the liberal rationalist policy of the caliphs al-Ma'mūn, al-Muʿtaṣim, and al-Wāthiq to the conservative traditionist policy of the Caliph al-Mutawakkil. However, al-Jāḥiẓ, though personally inclined toward the views of the former group, picked up on the winds of change and adapted to the new reality. He won over al-Mutawakkil's closest advisor, al-Fatḥ ibn Khāqān, a fellow bibliophile, and placated the caliph with his treatise *The Rebuttal of the Christians*, positioning himself as the exponent of a middle way between rational dialectic theology and literalist traditionalism. The epistle on the Turks, which was also completed during the reign of al-Mutawakkil, conforms well to this conservative agenda. Loyalty to the caliph and the stability of the regime are major themes of the epistle, and its unusually long opening address not only contains the standard praise of the patron but also devotes considerable attention to the importance of being a faithful subject and sincere adviser to the caliph, protecting him from adversaries and threats.

Historical Context and Significance[4]

The Abbasid dynasty that ruled the Islamic Empire during the lifetime of al-Jāḥiẓ had come to power in a revolution with the support of an army drawn chiefly from natives of the province of Khurasan, which spans modern eastern Iran, Turkmenistan, and western Afghanistan. Many of these Khurasani revolutionaries were from families with deep roots in this region, but a substantial number were the children or even grandchildren of Arab soldiers who had conquered the region and then taken up residence there and become assimilated to the local culture, marrying local women and adopting local customs. Both groups, therefore, identified as Khurasani. They marched east with the Abbasid leadership and, once victory was achieved, settled in Iraq, forming a major part of the imperial elite based in the new capital of Baghdad. Their offspring were known as "sons of the revolution," *abnā' al-dawlah* or just *abnā'*, or Banawis as al-Jāḥiẓ prefers to call them, and by and large they continued to be loyal to the Abbasid family and its government.

Matters remained relatively stable until the death of the Caliph Hārūn al-Rashīd in 193/809. However, the arrangements for his succession caused huge problems. He stipulated, in binding documents, that his first son, Muḥammad al-Amīn, should be caliph after him, and that the caliphate should then pass not to al-Amīn's sons, but to al-Rashīd's next two sons, ʿAbdallāh al-Ma'mūn and al-Qāsim al-Mu'taman, who should serve during al-Amīn's caliphate as governors of Khurasan and the Jazīrah (North Mesopotamia), respectively, including their frontier zones, without any interference from al-Amīn. The latter inevitably saw this as an excessive restriction on his authority as caliph, and immediately upon his father's death he sought to redraft the terms of the succession arrangement.

Over the course of the next two years, ever more heated negotiations were conducted; then, in early 195/811, as it became clear that no resolution was in sight, al-Amīn appointed his own governor of Khurasan and ordered the arrest of al-Ma'mūn, triggering an all-out civil war. Headquartered in Merv, the capital of Khurasan, al-Ma'mūn could draw on the support of the noble families of this rich and ancient province, many of whom had participated in the Abbasid revolution. A good example is his top general, Ṭāhir ibn Ḥuṣayn, who belonged to an aristocratic family of Bushang, near Herat, that had served the Abbasid family as soldiers and governors in this region for four generations.

Fighting on the opposite side, for al-Amīn, were the Banawis (Abnā'), who, though of Khurasani origin, had come to see Baghdad as their home and the caliph as the focus of their loyalty. The bitterness and ferocity of this civil war, which culminated in a siege of Baghdad and only ended with the death of al-Amīn in September 198/813, meant that Khurasanis and Banawis, who would previously have been comrades, now ended up on opposite sides of an acrimonious conflict.[5]

Al-Ma'mūn chose to stay in Merv for a further six years. This pleased his Khurasani allies, who now found themselves at the heart of the empire, but it irritated the Banawis, who had committed themselves to Baghdad. Another polarizing policy decision by al-Ma'mūn was his nomination of an ʿAlid (that is, a descendant of ʿAlī ibn Abī Ṭālib, the fourth caliph and son-in-law of the prophet Muḥammad) as his heir. This was acceptable to many in Khurasan, where Shiʿism had gained a firm hold through the eighth century, but it was anathema to the Banawis, whose loyalty and interests were closely tied to the Abbasids (descendants of the Prophet's uncle al-ʿAbbās).

As opposition grew, al-Ma'mūn realized he would have to change course if he hoped to remain caliph. The sudden death of his ʿAlid heir and the murder of his pro-Khurasani vizier, al-Faḍl ibn Sahl, precipitated his decision, and he set off for Baghdad in 203/819, making it once more the sole capital of the Islamic Empire. This certainly calmed the situation, but the animosity between the Khurasanis and Banawis still smoldered and caused much ill feeling within the Abbasid elite. This rancor forms the background to al-Jāḥiẓ's *The Turks*, and it is likely that he intended this treatise to assuage some of these resentments.

A second source of tension in the caliphal army was occasioned by the introduction of Turkish soldiers.[6] Our earliest report about this comes from the geographer and historian al-Yaʿqūbī (d. ca. 297/910), who tells us that, beginning around 200/815–16, al-Muʿtaṣim purchased Turks, many from Transoxiana via the governor of Samarqand, and others from private individuals in Baghdad. By the time of his brother's death and his own accession to the caliphate, he had acquired some three thousand, whom he had trained and employed as a private militia. Because they would often come into conflict with the citizens of Baghdad—riding at top speed on their horses and starting fights—al-Muʿtaṣim constructed a new settlement for them, called Samarra, about 80 miles (130 kilometers) upriver from Baghdad, where they could be kept separate from the local population. As well as accommodation for these troops, the new city provided space for palaces for their high-ranking officers and for the caliph himself, as well as for mosques, baths, markets, and the like.

The phenomenon of Turkish regiments acquired through purchase and serving as distinct units loyal to a single commander subsequently spread throughout the Muslim world. For this reason, there has been much debate over the origins and nature of the phenomenon. The most contentious issue is whether we should characterize these soldiers as slaves. On the one hand, they were acquired through purchase (they are often referred to as *mamlūk*s, which literally means "owned"), but on the other hand, they were subsequently freed and given stipends and weapons. Many went on to hold senior positions in the imperial army and even to become governors of provinces; they were powerful enough to threaten their leaders if they felt they were being mistreated, and they even killed four caliphs in the years 246–56/861–70. Therefore, some scholars—and I count myself as one of them—feel it muddies our understanding of slavery in the Islamic world if we put regular slaves, who could legitimately be handled as property, with all that entailed in terms of control and abuse, on a par with these soldiers, who would quickly turn on their masters if they treated them ill.[7] It would be like classifying modern professional soccer players, who are also acquired through purchase, on a par with persons trafficked for sex and labor. Certainly, al-Jāḥiẓ's treatise never gives the slightest hint of Turkish soldiers being regarded as slaves, not even to refute it as an erroneous and scurrilous opinion held by their detractors. Acquisition through purchase was, in this particular case, more about ensuring personal loyalty than about subjugation and enslavement.

A second contentious issue is whether it indicates a severe failing of the Islamic world that it had to buy in outsiders to manage security and defense.[8] This is a complex question, but it is again worth listening to what al-Jāḥiẓ says here, since he was not just a contemporary of these events, but, given his connections with al-Muʿtaṣim and al-Fatḥ ibn Khāqān, also had access to inside information. For him, the reason for adopting Turkish soldiers was obvious: They were brilliant horsemen, being born to the saddle in a region where horses and horsemanship were part of life, and they had learned to fight and shoot arrows with great dexterity while on horseback. This made them a formidable military asset, and so it was unsurprising that many leaders wanted to have them. Taking a broader view, one can see that from the fifth to the thirteenth century various steppe peoples of Central Asia—Huns, Gokturks, Khazars, Seljuks, Mongols, and so on—used their awesome equine skills to successfully challenge empires, which then had to respond by upgrading their cavalry regiments and so imported skilled equestrians by various means.

It is also important to bear in mind that, although al-Muʿtaṣim is retrospectively credited with inaugurating the Turkish slave-soldier system, he himself was simply following a practice adopted by numerous powerful military leaders in times of crisis—namely, acquiring a private militia. A famous example is the *bucellarii* of the Roman general Belisarius (d. AD 565), whom he recruited to counter a growing threat from Sasanian Iran and the Bulgars. Many of them were prisoners of war, offered their freedom in return for service to him, and this is also the case for the Bukhariyyah of the Umayyad governor ʿUbaydallāh ibn Ziyād (d. 67/686) and the Dhakwaniyyah of the Umayyad general Sulaymān ibn Hishām (d. 130/747).[9] Al-Ma'mūn's move to Merv afforded access to local leaders who had close dealings with the Turkic tribes in these frontier zones, and this provided opportunity. The chronic instability and rivalries created by the civil war and its chaotic aftermath supplied motive. We therefore do not need to posit a moral deficiency in Islamic society. These Turkish regiments gave a military advantage, and so their adoption is not so surprising in the context of the bitter and contentious civil war between al-Amīn and al-Ma'mūn. Once they had proved their worth, and as ever more Turkish tribes entered Muslim-ruled lands in the course of the third/ninth and fourth/tenth centuries, their deployment spread across the Islamic Empire.

A final and related issue is whether we should regard the "slave-soldier" system, or the mamluk institution as it is sometimes referred to, as "a peculiarly Islamic phenomenon" or a borrowing from outside. Most Islamic scholars tend to assume the former, but a few experts on Central Asia have suggested that it is an adoption, or at least an adaptation, of the Central Asian *shakar* system, whereby a group of elite soldiers is acquired by a "master," who forms a close relationship with them through a set of binding oaths and expectations.[10] We do not have sufficiently detailed information to decide this question, but it is a fascinating one, and it makes sense that, at a time when the caliphate was effectively based in Central Asia and supported by many Central Asian noble families, some of that region's military ethos and practices filtered through into Islamic military thinking.

Besides the Khurasanis, Banawis, and Turks, al-Jāḥiẓ refers to two other groups in the imperial army: Arabs and Mawlas. The former, especially tribesmen of Arabia, Syria, and the Jazīrah, had been the mainstay of the Umayyads, but their defeat by the Abbasids, who relied mainly on Khurasanis, had reduced the role of Arabs in the military.[11] Their inclusion in *The Turks* is more for historical reasons, though it is true that al-Amīn had recruited some Arab tribes of Syria and the Jazīrah in his fight with his brother. Mawla (Arabic: sg. *mawlā*, pl. *mawālī*) refers either to a freedman—that is, a slave or prisoner of war manumitted in return for certain benefits to the manumitter, commonly service for a specified period—or to a client, a free person who has become bound by mutual agreement to a patron and become a member of his household.[12] The tie between freedman and manumitter (*walā' al-ʿitq*) was a servile one—the former provided labor and the latter protection (he was required to pay blood money for the freedman, act as marriage guardian to his female dependents, and so on), but that between client and patron (*walā' al-muwālāt*) was a contract between two free parties, either of whom could terminate the arrangement. Whereas the freedman could be found in all areas of society, including the military, the client was more likely to be found in the upper echelons, and al-Jāḥiẓ clearly has in mind the clients of the caliph (*mawālī amīr al-mu'minīn*), since he talks of them as belonging to the Abbasids, living within the precincts of their palaces, and being educated with their children. Many of these caliphal clients were members of noble, even royal, families from Khurasan and Transoxiana. Some of them served as officers in the army, but more commonly they were courtiers and high-ranking bureaucrats, and this is perhaps why al-Jāḥiẓ does not say anything about their martial skills.

Literary Context and Significance[13]

The Turks and the Caliphal Army belongs to the genre of the *risālah*, an epistle on a specific topic and addressed to a particular person. The latter may have previously written a letter requesting the author to treat the subject in question, or it may be that something the addressee did provoked the author to pick up his pen and broach the matter on his own initiative. Al-Jāḥiẓ adopts this genre and gives it his own distinctive stamp. The addressees, even if they are persons whom he is genuinely corresponding with, become for him a rhetorical device. He uses them as a foil to argue against or as a mouthpiece to pose the questions he wishes to tackle. His attitude toward the addressee will also guide readers in deciding what position they should take toward the chosen topic. Crucially, the addressee will in some way be the means to a debate, which is al-Jāḥiẓ's favorite medium for exploring an issue, enabling him to present opposing sides of an argument or different perspectives on a controversy.

The Turks can be divided into two main parts. The first part opens with a preface in which al-Jāḥiẓ praises his addressee, al-Fatḥ ibn Khāqān, commending his concern and support for the caliph. Then he continues with the account of a conference on the composition and unity of the caliphal army convened by al-Fatḥ and attended by various members of the military and political elite. Al-Fatḥ argues that the five main component groups of the army are well integrated and interconnected, but an unnamed participant speaks against this contention, asserting that these groups were not at all united and were only held together by God's favor and intervention. He reinforces his point by describing the boasts and claims to superiority of each of the groups, though he leaves out the Turks. The second part contains al-Jāḥiẓ's attempt to remedy this omission, offering a series of anecdotal illustrations of the superiority of the Turks, some reported to him by informants and some that he himself had witnessed. He prefaces his contribution with a theoretical discussion of the subject, in the course of which he reveals that he had initially written on this topic for the Caliph al-Muʿtaṣim, but for reasons that he does not divulge it was never submitted to him, and he appends to it a short conclusion to wrap up the epistle.

It would be possible to envisage a historical scenario for the composition of *The Turks* along the following lines: Al-Jāḥiẓ had written a treatise on the Turks at the request of al-Muʿtaṣim, who needed to portray his deployment of them in a positive light to win over detractors. Circumstances changed and the treatise was no longer required or desired, and so al-Jāḥiẓ shelved it until sometime after 235/850, when he was approached with a similar request by al-Fatḥ ibn Khāqān. The latter had been engaged in a dispute about the composition of the caliphal army and needed some ammunition to bolster his position about the army's unity and the importance of the role of the Turks in its effective functioning. Al-Jāḥiẓ then dug out his mothballed treatise and repurposed it for his new patron, prefixing the first part, describing the encounter between al-Fatḥ and his opponent, and possibly adding other pertinent material, such as the exchange between al-Junayd and the Khāqān (§8).

Whether this historical reconstruction is true or not, it is nevertheless the case that considerable literary artifice has gone into the making of this text. The first part contains al-Jāḥiẓ's signature device, setting up a debate between two opposing parties. But the two sides of this debate are presented in very different ways. The thoughts of al-Fatḥ on the unity of the army are conveyed by al-Jāḥiẓ through paraphrase, summary, and indirect quotation. The views of al-Fatḥ's adversary, by contrast, are advanced via rhetorical speeches on behalf of the Khurasanis, Arabs, Mawlas, and Banawis. These speeches are conveyed as direct quotations, given largely in the first person, and are hortatory, expressing the boastful claims of these four groups to preeminence, each concluding with a plea for their group to be considered the best and most deserving in the caliphal army (§3.11, §3.15, §3.22, and §3.27). At the very least, al-Jāḥiẓ provides theoretical underpinning and justification to al-Fatḥ's stance and rhetorical fire to his antagonist's position. One suspects, though, that he supplies more than this. The way in which the two parties put forward their arguments is so different as to seem contrived. The aim is perhaps to win over the audience to the position of al-Fatḥ, backed up by calm and reasoned argument, which is clearly endorsed by al-Jāḥiẓ, against the position of the interlocutor, which is based on passionate and partisan boasting.

With the failure of the interlocutor to even mention the Turks, the stage is set for al-Jāḥiẓ to offer his own reflections on them. He starts by setting out how he will proceed, emphasizing that he will avoid a polemical and sectarian approach, that he seeks harmony and understanding rather than discord and disagreement, and that it would be wrong to extol the Turks only by disparaging others, all surely a dig at the strategy of al-Fatḥ's opponent. There follows an account of another debate, one that took place in Baghdad between several military leaders, who were asked by an emissary of the Caliph al-Ma'mūn whether they would rather face one hundred Turks or one hundred members of the Kharijite sect, who were feared for their unflinching valor and uncompromising religious principles. This gives the opportunity for one of the military chiefs to set out at length why it is that the Turks are the tougher enemy—tougher even than the Kharijites. The latter were evidently chosen here because they had been notorious since the early days of Islam for their ruthlessness and prowess, a corollary of their total devotion to their cause and their ascetic way of life, which permitted them to travel unencumbered by an army's usual material trappings.[14] That the Turks were better even than these dedicated warriors was a compliment indeed, and the rest of the treatise pushes home this superiority. The aim of all this praise is suggested by an observation al-Jāḥiẓ made to a friend when they were watching a parade of cavalry on a blazing hot day. The Turkish participants remained steadfast in their saddles, while the other horsemen flopped exhausted to the ground, prompting al-Jāḥiẓ to remark, "Al-Mu'taṣim certainly knew the Turks well when he enlisted them and attached them to himself" (§7.1), evidently intended as a ringing endorsement of al-Mu'taṣim's policy.

Al-Jāḥiẓ tells us that the Turks do, nevertheless, have one disadvantage: their longing for their homeland and their strong attachment to their ancestral customs (§§7.3–7.11). This gives al-Jāḥiẓ the chance to expatiate on two of his favorite themes, present in many of his works: nostalgia for one's native country and the effect of environment on character.[15] In the Turks, these two themes come together, since the Turks' temperament is particularly affected by "the characteristics of their land and their native soil and waters" (§7.4). Yet, though the Turks may experience this yearning more intensely than most, it is to some extent true for all humankind. When someone settles in a new place, after only one generation they and their offspring will have become assimilated to the character and mores of their new home. "The same applies in all lands," declares al-Jāḥiẓ. "You cannot distinguish between descendants of newcomers and descendants of indigenous inhabitants" (§7.5). This is in line with the theory of environmental determinism elaborated by Hippocrates in his *On Airs, Waters, and Places*, and was an aspect of the late antique worldview prevalent in the Middle East. It is very useful to al-Jāḥiẓ in this treatise, for it furthers his argument in two ways. First, it supports the idea that different peoples, such as the Khurasanis and Turks, have much in common, for "the lands that contain these peoples, even if not exactly corresponding, are substantially alike" (§2.2). Second, it corroborates the notion that peoples are shaped by their environment to excel at certain activities: the Greeks at philosophy and invention, the Chinese at manufacture and design, the Persians at statecraft, and the Turks at horsemanship and warfare (§§7.12–7.20).

A second major theme is the importance of fostering harmony and unity and of avoiding partisanship and division. In his report about the conference on the caliphal army, al-Jāḥiẓ explicitly attributes this conciliatory approach to the epistle's addressee, al-Fatḥ: "You asserted that the other speaker's objective was disharmony and the fostering of factionalism, whereas your aim was harmony and reconciliation" (§2.7) and "You declared that the relations between all the parts of the caliphal army are convergent, not divergent" (§2.10). In the methodological prelude to his own discussion of the Turks, he makes clear that his thinking aligns with that of al-Fatḥ: "We have only undertaken this work to reconcile hearts where they are discordant, to increase such mutual understanding as already exists, and to ascertain the essential unity of the various positions so that their opinions may be reconciled and their minds set at rest" (§4.1). He wants to be moderate and fair in his assessment, "not extravagant in the praise of one group and excessive in the abuse of others" (§4.10). And in his conclusion, al-Jāḥiẓ sums up his approach with the pithy saying: "Something small that unites is better than something big that creates dissension" (§9.2).

This theme of harmony brings us back again to the historical dimension of *The Turks*. For although this theme has overtones of the Aristotelian golden mean and the ordered equilibrium of God's creation, the treatise does appear to be rooted in the very live issue of al-Jāḥiẓ's day: the rifts in the caliphal army. I do not mean this in the sense that the treatise documents the events and debates of the time—the civil war between al-Amīn and al-Ma'mūn, the battle for Baghdad, the animosities provoked by the introduction of the Turks, al-Mutawakkil's machinations against some of the Turkish generals: None of these matters are discussed, even though al-Jāḥiẓ had lived through them. He is not and does not seek to be a chronicler, and yet he does have a message to impart. He wants to warn against the perils of factional strife and of fueling its fires, and he evidently does desire to mitigate its corrosive effects on the cohesion of the Abbasid regime. James Montgomery has described al-Jāḥiẓ's great work *The Book of Living* as "a palliative work written for a riven society,"[16] and the same could surely be said, if on a smaller scale, for *The Turks*.

He achieves this goal in part by making linkages across the groups—for example, Khurasanis and Turks are from the same eastern region, and Arabs and Turks are both descendants of Abraham—and in part by stressing that all the groups in their different ways have been crucial to the Abbasid cause. He highlights the glorious revolution, to which all parties bar the Turks contributed: The Khurasanis provided the missionaries and the bulk of the troops; the Arabs supplied most of the revolutionary leaders; the Mawlas were responsible for the two main architects, Abū Muslim and Abū Salamah; and the Banawis/ Abnā᾽ had their origins in the revolution and supported the Abbasid family that it installed on the caliphal throne. The Turks, though absent at the beginning, had now stepped up to defend the values of that revolution, to keep safe the Abbasid family, and to further their cause: "They have become a mighty army that is a mainstay for Islam, and a protection, a refuge, and an impregnable defense for the caliphs" (§7.24). And to a leader who recognizes their worth—a slight warning here—they will be totally loyal (§7.11). Al-Jāḥiẓ evidently thought that participation in the Abbasid revolution and loyalty to the Abbasid cause could be a rallying cry for all factions of the army: something that could unite them. At heart, al-Jāḥiẓ was very much a supporter of the Abbasid regime, and its stability was important to him.

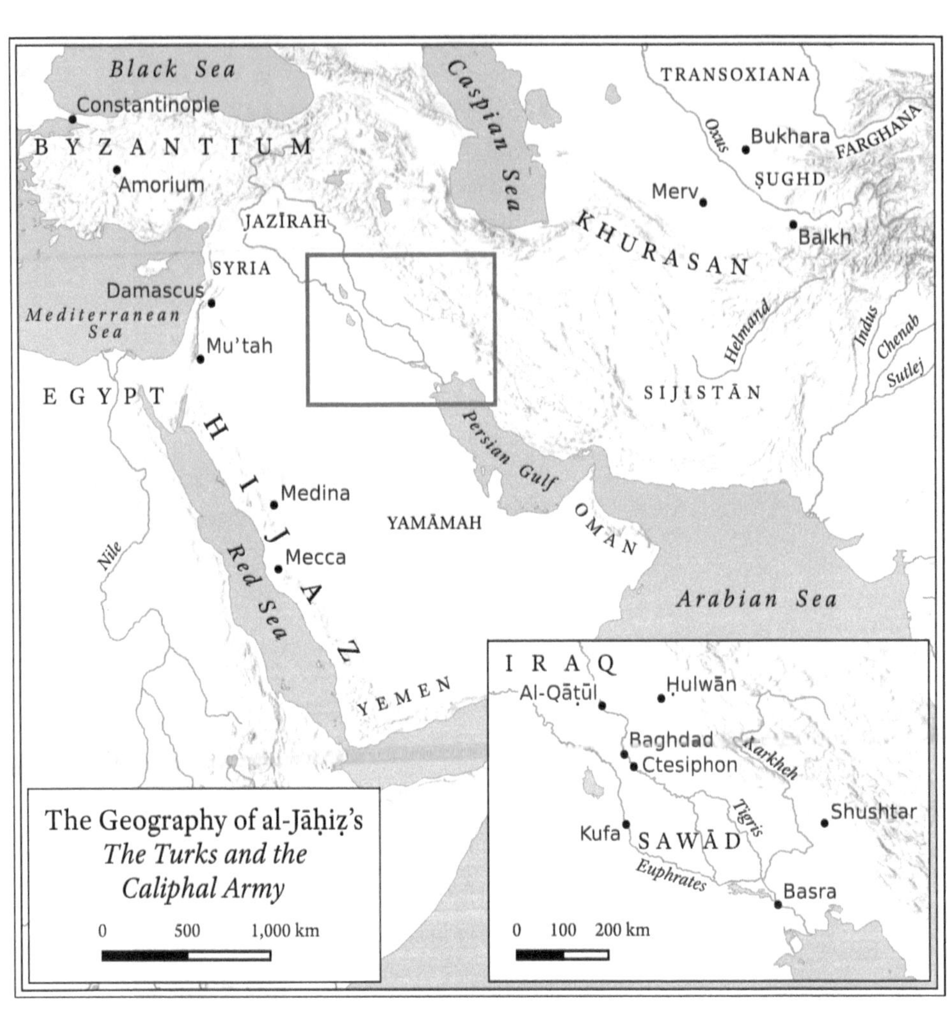

The Geography of al-Jāḥiẓ's *The Turks and the Caliphal Army*

Genealogical Tables

Table 1: From Noah to the Arabs and the Israelites

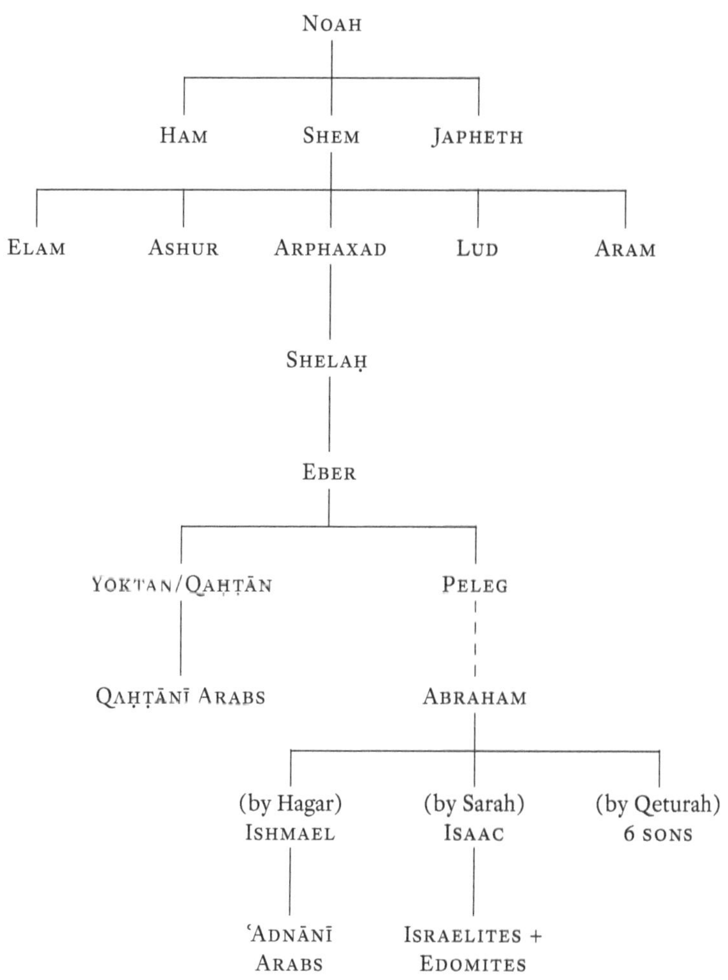

Table 2: From ʿAbd Manāf to the Umayyads and Abbasids

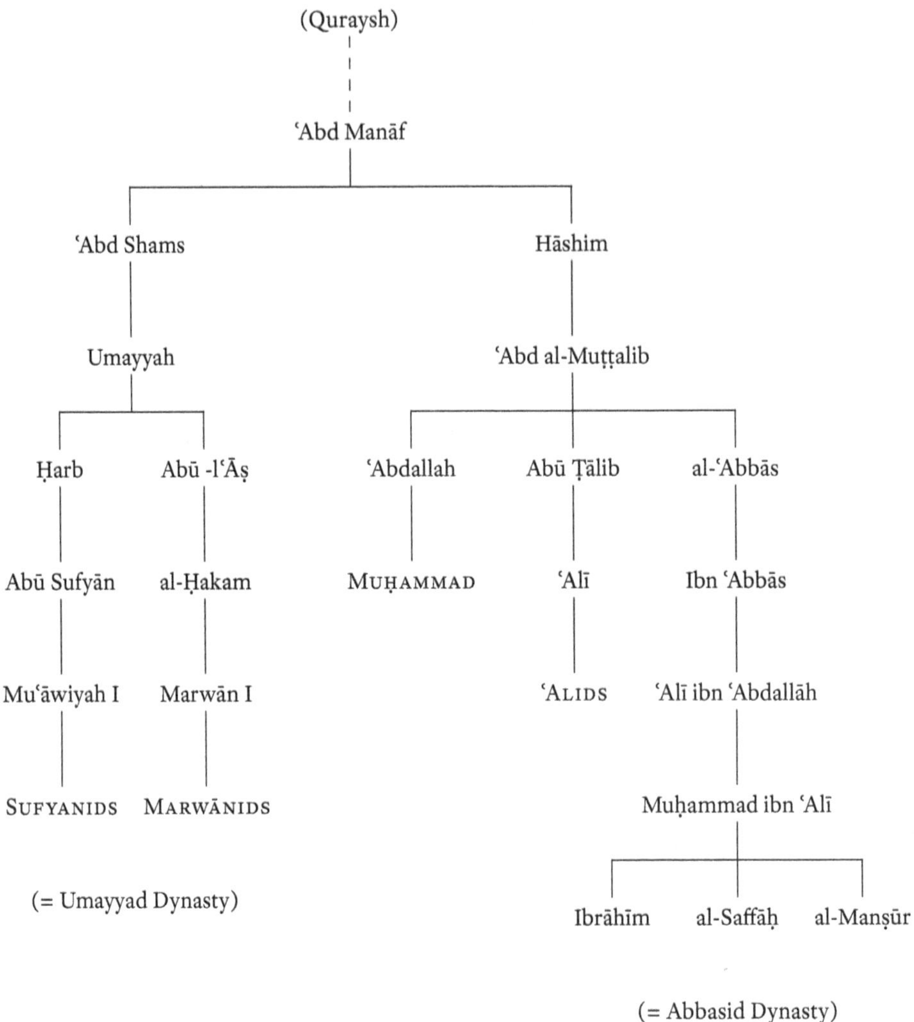

Note on the Text

The Edition

Manuscripts

Al-Jāḥiẓ's treatise *The Turks and the Caliphal Army* is preserved in two collections of his epistles. One collection, comprising seventeen epistles, is anonymous and is represented by the sixth-/twelfth-century manuscript Damad Ibrahim Pasha (Istanbul) 949 (D). Other witnesses to this collection exist, such as Suleimaniyye Ayasofia 4159 and Paris 6013, but they are almost identical to D, and so I will not refer to them in this edition. The second collection, comprising twenty-nine epistles, was assembled by a certain ʿUbaydallāh ibn Ḥassān and was written down in 403/1013 according to the manuscripts that preserve this collection.[17] The earliest extant witness to it is found in MS Emanet Hazinesi (Topkapi Palace, Istanbul) 1358 of the eleventh/seventeenth century (T), which I use as the basis for my edition.[18]

There is also a group of Egyptian manuscripts that transmit ʿUbaydallāh's collection. They are so close to one another in wording that they must rely, directly or indirectly, on a single manuscript copied in the thirteenth/nineteenth century in al-Qāhirah (Cairo), which I shall label Q. The principal members of this group are as follows:

- British Library Or. 3138 (London), formerly Rieu suppl. 1129, copied in Cairo for the Austrian scholar Baron Von Kraemer in 1877 (L)
- Jāmiʿat al-Azhar 6836, dated 1313/1895 (J)
- Dār al-Kutub al-Miṣriyyah, 19 adab Taymur, dated 1315/1897 (M), copied by the same scribe as J
- A copy of the epistles written in the margin of an edition of al-Mubarrad's *Kāmil* printed in Cairo in 1323/1908 (K)

T and Q are very close, but there are a few small differences, and T occasionally has a reading that is the same as D but different from Q.

The versions of *The Turks* in these two collections, as represented by D and T-Q, differ in several respects. Most notably, each of the two versions is missing some text that is present in the other. Thus, D lacks

§3.13 line 2 (الذين لا يتّكلون) – §3.23 line 3 (وبصّر من العمى)
§3.24 line 2 (ولنا معانقة الأبطال) – §3.27 line 2 (تبع لها وكذلك)

And T-Q lacks

§4.15 line 1 (وقد قال النابغة) – §4.19 line 4 (حَتَّى تَجَلَّتِ)
§5.21 line 2 (ولا تكون المقانب) – §7.7 line 4 (ضرب به قتيبة المثل)
§7.22 line 1 (قال ثمّ إنّ الترك عطفت) – §8.16 line 6 (وكلّها جواد)

One might at first think that these two versions of the epistle represent al-Jāḥiẓ's earlier and later renditions—the one he says he drafted for al-Muʿtaṣim (§4.13) and the one he addressed to al-Fatḥ ibn Khāqān. However, though al-Jāḥiẓ may well have produced two or more redactions of his epistle on the Turks, the two versions of it that survive in our manuscripts clearly belong to the same redaction. Where the two versions overlap, they do not differ in any major way, and are indeed quite close in wording, although there are many occasions where one version has a few words not present in the other version. There are also numerous small differences in word choice, a substantial proportion of which look as though they are due to variant readings of the same original words; for example: مناول/منازل (§1.3), اخابير/اجناس (§1.5), تهجم/تهكم (§2.1), بغنم/يقيم (§5.5), النظر بالعودة/البصر بالعورة (§5.7), سير/سنن (§5.16), and عادات/غارات (§5.19).

In short, we should not assume that al-Jāḥiẓ produced a single finished version of *The Turks*; by his own admission, he reworked this epistle on at least two occasions in his lifetime. Yet we can be reasonably sure that both versions of the extant text of *The Turks*, in D and T-Q, derive from the same form of the epistle, which is plausibly the latest incarnation of it, certainly later than the draft of it that al-Jāḥiẓ says he composed for al-Muʿtaṣim. However, this positive assessment is tempered by the fact that the two anthologists who included it in their respective collections of al-Jāḥiẓ's epistles felt free to abridge it and to revise its wording. We therefore only have *The Turks* in a mediated form, reshaped to some extent by its transmitters. The distinctiveness of al-Jāḥiẓ's language and style nevertheless shines through and gives us some degree of confidence that this text substantially reflects al-Jāḥiẓ's own creative endeavor.

Previous Editions

There are three major modern editions of *The Turks*:

1. In van Vloten, *Tria opuscula*, 1–56, who referred to his manuscript sources by the letters A, B, and C. His A and B came from MS Leiden Arab. 7014, which is a copy of Paris 6013 (van Vloten's A) with collations from D (van Vloten's B). His C was MS Leiden Arab. 7016, which is a copy of L.[19] He blended readings from the three manuscripts and amended them as he saw fit. A copy of this edition was included in the collection of eleven treatises of al-Jāḥiẓ published by Muhammad Efendi al-Sāsī in Cairo at the Saʿādah Press in 1324/1906.
2. In ʿAbd al-Salām Hārūn, *Rasāʾil al-Jāḥiẓ*, volume 1, 1–86, based on D, but with reference also to L and K, as well as to the editions of van Vloten and al-Sāsī.
3. In ʿAbd al-Salām Hārūn, *Rasāʾil al-Jāḥiẓ*, volume 3, 163–220, based on Q (as witnessed by L, M, and K), but with reference also to his own earlier edition and to those of van Vloten and al-Sāsī.

This Edition

All the modern editors have dealt with the problem of the missing passages in the same way; that is, they have produced a maximalist edition, taking the passages not found in their base manuscript from a manuscript that does contain them. Although these editors do not explain their decision, it does seem a reasonable course of action, since the passages found in only one of the versions of the epistle do not differ in style from the passages present in both versions of the epistle, and they do not seem out of place. This makes it more likely that the two anthologists of al-Jāḥiẓ's epistles abbreviated rather than augmented their source text, each omitting some passages. I have therefore followed the practice of these earlier editors and provided a maximalist edition of the epistle on the Turks. However, I have deviated from their example in two ways. First, I take T as my base manuscript, in part because it has never been used before (presumably because it was difficult to access until relatively recently), and in part because it is the earliest representative of ʿUbaydallāh ibn Ḥassān's collection of al-Jāḥiẓ's epistles, which is fuller, and arguably better, than the collection preserved in D. Second, in line with LAL policy, I have been less interventionist in my editing; where previous editors have often emended their base manuscript and favored readings from other manuscripts, I have provided a largely faithful rendering of T, except for including the additional material that is only present in D, as noted above, and accepting the following minor emendations of van Vloten:

§1.5: صغوه instead of صغره.
§2.3: الحزون instead of الحزان.
§3.9: تجفافنا instead of أخفافنا.
§5.21: النهبة instead of الهيبة.

It is LAL policy to refer in the critical apparatus only to major variants, and so I have omitted those variants that do not greatly affect the meaning of the text, such as orthographical variations, use of different forms of the same root of a word, and use of synonyms, copying errors, and the like. I began by producing a comprehensive critical edition, and then proceeded to strip out the minor variants, but I hope to make the full edition available via the LAL website in due course.

Sigla

T/ت	Emanet Hazinesi 1358, Topkapi Palace, Istanbul
D/د	Damad Ibrahim Pasha 949, Istanbul
Q/ق	Cairene source of L, J, M, K
L/ل	British Library Or. 3138, London
J/ج	Jāmiʿat al-Azhar 6836
M/م	Dār al-Kutub al-Miṣriyyah, 19 adab Taymur
K/ك	*Kāmil* of al-Mubarrad, edition of Cairo 1323/1908, text written on margin

The Translation

Previous Translations

There is an English translation of this epistle by Harley Walker and a German one by Oskar Rescher.[20] Both relied only on van Vloten's edition—directly in Rescher's case and via the reprint of al-Sāsī in Harley Walker's case—and are quite literal. Moreover, Rescher omits many portions of the text, including the whole of the preface and "all the repetitions that present in different form the same idea with all manner of rhetorical embellishments, but without adding any substantively new meaning at all."[21] A more recent English translation by William Hutchins relies on the edition of Hārūn, volume 1, and was done with reference to Harley Walker's translation.[22] Only minimal annotation is given in these three translations and no introduction to the historical and literary context is provided.

This Translation

I began this translation in collaboration with Freddie Beeston, who sided with an approach usually called foreignization or exoticization, where the reader is encouraged to move some way toward the original author's style and worldview.[23] However, I have ended it with the Library of Arabic Literature, which favors the domestication or naturalization approach, where the author's text is reworked into a form closer to the reader's standpoint—that is, it is rendered immediately intelligible to the modern English reader.[24] Given LAL's mission to make Arabic literature more widely accessible, a more domesticizing approach certainly makes sense, and so I have revised the 1995 draft composed by Freddie and myself in that direction, with some much-appreciated help from the external reviewer. Yet, the gap is wide between contemporary English and classical Arabic, which makes this a difficult task. In particular, it is complicated by the penchant in Arabic literature for parallelism,[25] which al-Jāḥiẓ elevated to an art form. In Arabic, this is called *izdiwāj*—that is, saying the same thing twice but using different words or different forms of the same word. It is considered good literary style in Arabic, but is not easy to convey in English. One can collapse the two phrases into one, and I have often done this where the meaning of the two words or phrases is very close, combining them into a single phrase accompanied by an intensive adjective or adverb (for example, "I am delighted to see you and pleased to behold you" may be rendered as "I am very pleased to see you"). But often there is an appreciable difference in the sense or impact of the two words or phrases, and in such cases I have maintained the coupling and tried to convey the distinction between its components in the translation.

A second difficulty is that al-Jāḥiẓ's sentences are often lengthy and intricate, a reflection of his style of thought. As Beeston put it: "Hardly has any idea presented itself to his consciousness before he rambles off into a series of observations, adding to it or qualifying it, and these may lead in the end to a near contradiction of the remark which started the train of thought off."[26] To render such a manner of writing into readable English means striking a fine balance: One must sometimes break up these long sentences and untangle their strands while still trying to convey some impression of the original structures and thought processes.

The two aforementioned difficulties are the most commented upon in translations of al-Jāḥiẓ, but more challenging for me was what one might call his informal formality or ponderous levity. By this I mean that he frequently expresses quite weighty observations in elegantly simple and concise language. For example, at the end of section 1.2, al-Jāḥiẓ says, in explanation of why more people talk about doing good than actually do it: "*thawābu l-ʿamal muʾajjal wa-ḥtimālu mā fīhi muʿajjal.*" Literally, this means: "the reward of action is delayed, whereas the bearing of what is in it [i.e., what it entails] is hastened." It is easy to understand what the phrase means in Arabic, but its beautifully neat concision, which will elicit admiration from devotees of classical Arabic, is hard to convey in English. It also includes a nice sound play in the words *muʾajjal* and *muʿajjal*—a common device in al-Jāḥiẓ but, again, a nightmare to replicate in English without sounding stilted. Preferring to privilege clarity, I have opted for an interpretative translation: "the reward for good works comes only after some time, whereas the effort involved in their accomplishment must be borne immediately." This captures quite well the sense of al-Jāḥiẓ's expression, but not its graceful succinctness, and for this failing I apologize in advance.

A Note on Transliteration

Finally, in keeping with the Library of Arabic Literature's preference for avoiding "mixed" transliterations—words marked with diacritics as though they were transliterated Arabic but that are also given English-language elements, such as a final "s" plural—macrons, dotted letters, and half-rings are not used for any Arabic term that appears in both singular and plural forms in the text (such as Banawi/Banawis, Mawla/Mawlas, and Khurasani/Khurasanis). An Arabic term that appears only in the singular in the text is fully transliterated, as in Yamāmī, Ibāḍī, and Jazarī.

Notes to the Introduction

1 The classic work on the life and times of al-Jāḥiẓ is Pellat's *Le milieu Baṣrien et la formation de Ǧāḥiẓ*; also useful is his anthology *The Life and Works of Jāḥiẓ*. On al-Jāḥiẓ's addressees in general, see Hefter, *The Reader in al-Jāḥiẓ*, ch. 1 ("The Addressee and the Occasion of Writing"), and Schoeler, "Writing for a Reading Public: The Case of al-Jāḥiẓ."

2 El-Hibri, "Tabari's Biography of al-Mu'tasim: The Literary Use of a Military Career"; Gordon, "The Khāqānid Families of the Early Abbasid Period," 239–41.

3 This is a huge subject, but for an easy introduction see Bennison, *The Great Caliphs*, ch. 5 ("Baghdad's 'Golden Age'"). On the emergence of a literary culture in al-Jāḥiẓ's time, see Toorawa, *Ibn Abī Ṭāhir Ṭayfūr and Arabic Writerly Culture*; on the translation movement, see Gutas, *Greek Thought, Arabic Culture*; and for some thoughts on the theological context, see van Ess, "Al-Jāḥiẓ and Early Mu'tazilī Theology."

4 Although a little dated now, two helpful guides to this subject are Kennedy, *The Early Abbasid Caliphate*, and Lassner, *The Shaping of Abbasid Rule*.

5 See further Crone, "The 'Abbāsid Abnā' and Sāsānid Cavalrymen," and Turner, "The *abnā' al-dawla*: The Definition and Legitimation of Identity in Response to the Fourth Fitna."

6 The most accessible overview to this topic is provided by Gordon, *The Breaking of a Thousand Swords*.

7 I am not interested so much in whether they "really" were slaves or not (certainly the standard vocabulary of slavery is also applied to them, though such terms are relational, and all are slaves before God and the ruler), but whether it is useful for our understanding of the phenomenon and of Islamic society to view them as such.

8 This is the moral bankruptcy theory of Patricia Crone's *Slaves on Horses*, which postulates, in brief, that the Abbasid regime became regarded as illegitimate by the religious establishment and so found it difficult to recruit sufficient fighting men, and because of this it had to turn to slaves.

9 Athamina, "Non-Arab Regiments and Private Militias During the Umayyad Period."

10 In particular, see de la Vaissière, *Samarcande à Samarra*.

11 On the elaboration of a distinctive Arab identity in the early Islamic period, see Webb, *Imagining the Arabs*.

12 For a recent study of this phenomenon, see Urban, *Conquered Populations in Early Islam.*

13 Studies of *The Turks* appear in McDonald, "Al-Ǧāḥiẓ and His Analysis of the Turks"; Lassner, *The Shaping of Abbasid Rule*, ch. 5; Gabrieli, "La *risāla* di al-Ǧāḥiẓ sui Turchi"; and Hefter, *The Reader in al-Jāḥiẓ*, 148–62.

14 For a recent study of this feared sect of Islam, see Hagemann, *The Kharijites in Early Islamic Historical Tradition: Heroes and Villains.*

15 Hefter, *The Reader in al-Jāḥiẓ*, ch. 3 ("Undisclosed Origins and Homelands").

16 Montgomery, *Al-Jāḥiẓ: In Praise of Books*, 265.

17 The copying is ascribed in the manuscripts to one ʿUbaydallāh ibn ʿAlī. Pellat ("Nouvel essai d'inventaire de l'oeuvre ǧāḥiẓienne," 119) maintains that this person should be identified with ʿUbaydallāh ibn Ḥassān and that the collection itself was made in 403/1013, but Hārūn argues that they are two persons and that ʿUbaydallāh ibn ʿAlī copied in 403/1013 the collection of ʿUbaydallāh ibn Ḥassān, which was therefore made before 403/1013. The Arabic verb used here (كتب) could mean either copied or composed.

18 Described in Şeşen, "Câḥiẓ'in eserlerinin Istanbul kütüphanelerindeki yazma nüshalari ve bunlar hakkinda bazi yeni malzameler," 124–28.

19 Van Vloten does not give this information himself (he committed suicide before writing an introduction to his edition), but it is supplied by Vorhoeve, *Handlist of Arabic Manuscripts in the Library of the University of Leiden*, 284.

20 Harley Walker, "Jahiz of Basra to Al-Fath ibn Khaqan on 'The Exploits of the Turks and the Army of the Khalifate in General'"; Rescher, "Das Schreiben des Dschâhiz an el-Fath ibn Khâqân, den Wezîr des khalifen el-Mutawakkil über 'Die Vorzüge der Türken.'"

21 Rescher, "Das Schreiben," 107n.

22 Hutchins, *Nine Essays of al-Jahiz*, 175–218; he acknowledges his debt to Hārūn and Harley Walker on page 219.

23 E.g., Beeston, "Review of: Nine Essays of al-Jahiz by W. M. Hutchins," 200.

24 For a recent discussion of this old issue, see Venuti, *The Translator's Invisibility.*

25 On this phenomenon, see Beeston, "Parallelism in Arabic Prose."

26 Beeston, *The Epistle on Singing-Girls by Jāḥiẓ*, 1.

الرسالة إلى الفتح بن خاقان في مناقب الترك وعامّة جند الخلافة

The Turks and the Caliphal Army

١،١ وفّقك الله وأرشدك وأعان على شكرك وأصلحك وأصلح على يديك وجعلنا وإيّاك ممّن يقول بالحقّ ويعمل به ويؤثره ويحتمل ما فيه ممّا قد يصدّ عنه ولا يكون حظّه الوصف له والمعرفة به دون الحثّ عليه والانقطاع إليه وكشف القناع فيه وإيصاله إلى أهله والصبر على المحافظة في أن لا يصل إلى غيرهم والتثبّت في تحقيقه لديهم فإنّ الله تعالى لم يعلّم الناس ليكونوا عالمين دون أن يكونوا عاملين وإنّما علّمهم ليعملوا وبيّن لهم ليتّقوا

٢،١ ولخوف الوقوع في المضارّ والتوسّط في المهالك طلب الناس التبيّن[١] ولحبّ السلامة من الهلكة والرغبة في المنفعة احتملوا ثقل العلم وتعجّلوا مكروه المعاناة ولقلّة العاملين وكثرة الواصفين قال الأوّلون العارفون أكثر من الواصفين والواصفون أكثر من العاملين[٢] وإنّما كثرت الصفات وقلّت الموصوفات لأنّ ثواب العمل مؤجّل واحتمال ما فيه معجّل

٣،١ وقد أعجبني ما رأيت من شغفك بطاعة إمامك واحتجاجك لتدبير خليفتك وإشفاقك من كلّ خلل يدخله[٣] وإن دقّ ونال سلطانه وإن صغر ومن كلّ أمر خالف هواه وإن خفي مكانه وجانب رضاه وإن قلّ ضرره ومن تخوّفك أن يجد المنازل[٤] إليه متطرّقًا والعدوّ عليه متعلّقًا

٤،١ فإنّ السلطان لا ينفكّ من متأوّل ناقم ومن محكوم عليه ساخط ومن معزول عن الحكم زار ومن متعطّل متصفّح ومن معجب برأيه ذي خطل في بيانه مولع

١ ولخوف . . . التبيّن: ق: التورّط في وسط الخوف والوقوع في المضارّ والتوسّط في المهالك فلذالك طلب الناس التبيين. ٢ قال . . . العاملين: د: كثرت الصفات وقلّت الموصوفات فإنّ الواصفين أكثر من العاملين.
٣ من كلّ خلل يدخله: د: من كلّ خلل وخلّة دخل على ملكه. ٤ ق: المتاوّل.

Part I

Address to al-Fatḥ ibn Khāqān

May God direct and guide you, encourage you to be thankful, make you prosper, and make others prosper through you. May He place both of us among those who proclaim the truth and act on it, who seek it out and endure what it entails against any obstacle. May our contribution to the truth be not only clear acknowledgment, but also exhortation of others to apply themselves to uncovering it. May we constantly ensure that the truth reaches its devotees, but not its detractors, and persist in its fulfillment among the former. For God did not teach men in order that they should know things without also being ready to act on them; rather, He taught them in order that they might conduct themselves appropriately and explained matters to them so that they might be God-fearing. 1.1

It is for fear of falling into harm's way and becoming embroiled in perilous situations that men have aimed at careful scrutiny of their affairs, and it is out of a desire to be safe from ruin and a craving for material gain that they take on the burden of learning and run after hateful toil. Because there are few who do good deeds and many who just talk about them, the ancients coined the saying, "More people know what is right than speak of it and more speak of it than do it." And the reason why there is more talk than action is simply that the reward for good works comes only after some time, whereas the effort involved in their accomplishment must be borne immediately. 1.2

I admire your evident enthusiasm for obedience to the Ruler[1] and advocacy of his policy, as well as your anxious care against any oversight, however insignificant, that might in any way impair his authority, and against any matter that might oppose his will or sidetrack his wishes, no matter how slight its effect or minimal its detriment. I also admire your solicitousness lest an opponent find a way to him or an enemy latch onto him. 1.3

For the Ruler can never be free of vengeful critics or failed petitioners bearing a grudge, of men removed from power who seek to find fault or unemployed busybodies, or of conceited chatterboxes eager to run down correct 1.4

بتهجين الصواب وبالاعتراض على التدبير حتّى كأنّه رائد لجميع الأمّة ووكيل لسكّان جميع المملكة يضع نفسه في مواضع الرقباء وفي مواضع التصفّح على الخلفاء والوزراء لا يعذر وإن كان مجاز العذر ظاهرًا ولا يقف فيما يكون للشكّ محتملاً ولا يصدّق بأنّ الشاهد يرى ما لا يرى الغائب وأنّه لا يعرف مصادر الرأي من لم يشهد موارده ومستدبره من لم يعرف مستقبله ومن محروم قد أضغنه الحرمان ومن لئيم قد أفسده الإحسان ومن مستبطئ قد أخذ أضعاف حقّه وهو لجهله بقدره ولضيق ذرعه وقلّة شكره يظنّ أنّ الذي بقي له أكثر ولحقّه أوجب ومن مستزيد لو ارتجع السلطان سالف أياديه البيض عنده ونعمته السالفة عليه لكان لذلك أهلاً وله مستحقًّا قد غرّه الإملاء وأبطره دوام الكفاية وأفسده طول الفراغ ومن صاحب فتنة خامل في الجماعة رئيس في الفرقة نعّاق في الهرج قد أقصاه عنه السلطان وأقام صغوه ثقاف الأدب وأذلّه الحكم بالحقّ فهو مغيظ لا يجد غير التشنيع ولا يتشفّى بغير الإرجاف ولا يستريح إلّا إلى الأماني ولا يأنس إلّا بكلّ مرجف كذّاب ومفتون مرتاب وخارص لا خير فيه وخالف لا غناء عنده يريد أن يسوّى بالكفاة ويرفع فوق الحماة لأمر سلف له ولإحسان كان من غيره وليس ممّن يربّ قديم مجد ولا يحفل بدروس شرف ولا يفصل بين ثواب المحتسبين وبين الحفظ لأبناء[1] المحسنين وكيف يعرف فرق ما بين حقّ الذمام وثواب الكفاية من لا يعرف طبقات الحقّ في مراتبه ولا يفصل بين طبقات الباطل في منازله

٥،١ ثمّ أعلم بعد ذلك أنّك بنفسك بدأت في تعظيم إمامك والحفظ بمناقب أنصار خليفتك وإيّاها حطت بحياطتك لأشياعه واحتجاجك لأوليائه ونعم العون أنت

١ المحتسبين . . . لأبناء: زيدت من د.

policy and raise objections to plans as if they were the public's watchdog and the people's representative, setting themselves up as supervisors charged with scrutinizing caliphs and viziers. Such a person makes no apology, even though one may be clearly called for; he does not hesitate in situations that admit the probability of a doubt; he does not accept that the testimony of an eyewitness outweighs that of those not present, and that nobody can understand the issues of a policy unless he is involved in its formulation, nor where it will lead unless he knows where it began. And the Ruler can never be rid of persons debarred from court and embittered by exclusion, or ignoble individuals spoiled by favor, or those who complain of their rights being overdue when they have already received them several times over and who, out of ignorance of their own worth, limited abilities, and insufficient gratitude, fancy that there is still more owed and that their claims are compelling. Nor can the Ruler escape greedy supplicants, who would fully deserve it if the Ruler were to demand the return of the great favors earlier bestowed, for they have become deluded and rendered haughty by the constant satisfaction of all their wants and corrupted by long idleness; or seditious troublemakers, unknown to wider society but leaders of a faction, always raising their voices at riots, and kept at arm's length by the Ruler, their waywardness reined in by the correcting rule of discipline and humbled by just judgment. Consequently, they are angry and find an outlet in denunciation and satisfaction in spreading falsehoods. They are only content with impossible aspirations and only associate with lying rumormongers or suspect insurgents, good-for-nothing slanderers or worthless backbiters. They seek to put themselves on a level with the truly worthy and be exalted over the heads of the guardians of state because of some service they had done long ago or even because of a deed performed by another. They are not the kind to nurture ancient glory or be concerned with the waning of honorable status; they make no distinction between the reward due to those who earn it and the mere memory that pertains to the descendants of benefactors. Yet how can the distinction between rights owed to someone protected by contract and the reward due to those who have performed public service be appreciated[2] if the distinction between the various gradations of true worth and of illusory worth is not understood?

I note that you, by contrast, personally took the initiative in reinforcing 1.5
the Ruler's glory and upholding his helpers' virtues, safeguarding him by your protection of his aides and defense of his friends. How helpful you can be, God

إن شاء الله على ملازمة الطاعة والموازرة على الخير والكفاية لأهل الحقّ وقد استدللت بالذي أرى من شدّة عنايتك وفرط اكتراثك وتفقّدك لأخابير الأعداء وبحثك عن مناقب الأولياء على أنّ ما ظهر من نصحك أمم في جنب ما بطن من إخلاصك فأمتع الله بك خليفته ومنحنا وإيّاك محبّته وأعاذنا وإيّاك من قول الزور والتقرّب بالباطل إنّه حميد مجيد فعّال لما يريد

١،٢ وذكرت أبقاك الله أنّك جالست أخلاطًا من جند الخلافة وجماعات من أبناء الدعوة وشيوخًا من جلّة الشيعة وكهولاً من أبناء رجال الدولة والمنسوبين إلى الطاعة والمناصحة ومحبّة الدينونة دون محبّة الرغبة والرهبة وأنّ رجلاً من عرض تلك الجملة[١] ارتجل الكلام ارتجال مستبدّ وتفرّد به تفرّد معجب وأنّه لم يستأمر زعماءهم ولم يراقب خطباءهم[٢] وأنّه تعسّف المعاني وتهجّم على الألفاظ وزعم أنّ جند الخلافة اليوم على خمسة أقسام خراسانيّ وتركيّ ومولى وعربيّ وبنويّ وأنّه أكثر من حمد الله وشكره على إحسانه ومننه وعلى جميع أياديه وسابغ نعمه وعلى شمول عافيته وجزيل مواهبه حين ألّف على الطاعة هذه القلوب المختلفة والأجناس المتباينة والأهواء المتفرّقة

٢،٢ وأنّك اعترضت على هذا المتكلّم المستبدّ وعلى هذا القائل المتكلّف الذي قسّم هذه الأقسام وخالف بين هذه الأركان وفصّل بين أنسابهم وفرّق بين أجناسهم وباعد بين أنسابهم[٣] وأنّك أنكرت ذلك عليه أشدّ الإنكار وقذعته أشدّ القذع وزعمت أنّهم لم يخرجوا من الاتّفاق أو من شيء يقرب من الاتّفاق وأنّك نفيت التباعد في النسب والتباين في السبب وقلت بل أزعم أنّ الخراسانيّ والتركيّ أخوان وأنّ الحيز واحد وأنّ حكم ذلك الشرق والقضيّة على ذلك الصقع متّفق غير مختلف

١ تلك الجملة: د: تلك الجماعة ومن حاشية الجلّة. ٢ وأنّه لم . . . خطباءهم: زيدت من د. ٣ وفرّق . . . أنسابهم: زيدت من د.

willing, in maintaining unswerving loyalty, promoting the public good, and supporting right-minded people. I conclude from what I see of the extreme care you take—the attention you pay to reports about enemies and your investigation into the qualities of friends—that your good counsel, apparent to all, pales in comparison with your inner sincerity. May God prosper His Ruler by your presence, grant us both His love, and deliver us both from lying speech and the currying of favor by means of falsehood. God is to be praised and glorified; He does what He wills.

The Argument of al-Fatḥ for the Unity of the Army

You, may God preserve you, mentioned that you held a conference with various members of the caliphal army and a good number of those active in the Abbasid cause, together with noble elders of the ruling party, senior statesmen, and those known for loyalty, good counsel, and the devotion inspired by religion and not by self-seeking or fear. Among those present at that assembly was a certain individual who delivered an ill-prepared and opinionated speech, expressing his own vain thinking and paying no heed or attention to any of the leading spokesmen before him. He impetuously poured out a muddle of ideas to the effect that the caliphal army of today consists of five separate elements: Khurasanis, Turks, Mawlas, Arabs, and Banawis.[3] Moreover, he made the exaggerated claim that it was only thanks to God's gracious benevolence, His abundant blessings and favors, and His all-encompassing bountiful protection that such varied dispositions and such diverse ethnic elements with their individually distinct prejudices had been combined into a common loyalty. 2.1

You, however, opposed this opinionated and pretentious speaker, who made such divisions and distinctions between these key elements of the army and their mutual connections and argued for the incompatibility of their genealogical and racial sentiments. You completely rejected and cast scorn on this view, maintaining that they have never lacked uniformity, or at any rate something very close to uniformity, and you denied any marked differentiation in their genealogical relationships. Rather, you said, you would argue that the Khurasani and the Turk are brothers, hailing from the same territory, and that the government and administration of that eastern region is harmonious and consistent. Their lines of descent, even though they may not be rooted in a 2.2

ومتقارب غير متفاوت وأنّ الأعراق في الأصل إلّا تكن كانت راسخة فقد كانت متشابهة وحدود البلاد المشتملة عليهم إن لا تكن متساوية فإنّها متناسبة وكلّهم خراسانيّ في الجملة وإن تميّزوا ببعض الخصائص وافترقوا ببعض الوجوه

٣،٢ وزعمت أنّ اختلاف التركيّ والخراسانيّ ليس كالاختلاف بين العجميّ والعربيّ ولا[1] كاختلاف ما بين الروميّ والصقلبيّ والزنجيّ والحبشيّ فضلاً على ما هو أبعد جوهرًا وأشدّ خلافًا بل كاختلاف ما بين المدريّ والوبريّ[2] والبدويّ والحضريّ والسهليّ والجبليّ[3] وكاختلاف ما بين من نزل البطون وبين من نزل الحزون[4] وبين من نزل النجود وبين من نزل الأغوار

٤،٢ وزعمت أنّ هؤلاء وإن اختلفوا في بعض اللغة وفارق بعضهم بعضًا في بعض الصورة فقد نجد أنّ عليا تميم وسفلى قيس وعجز هوازن وفصحاء الحجاز في اللغة وهي في أكثرها على[5] خلاف لغة حمير وسكّان مخاليف اليمن وكذلك الصورة والصورة والشمائل والأخلاق والأخلاق وكلّهم مع ذلك عربيّ خالص غير مشوب ولا معلهج ولا مذرّع ولا مزجّ ولم يختلفوا كاختلاف ما بين قحطان وعدنان من قبل ما طبع الله عليه تلك البريّة من خصائص الغرائز وما قسم لأهل كلّ جيرة من الشكل والصورة ومن الأخلاق واللغة

٥،٢ فإن قلت كيف صار أولادهما جميعًا عربًا مع اختلاف الأبوّة قلنا إنّ الجزيرة لمّا كانت واحدة فاستووا في التربة وفي اللغة وفي الشمائل والهمّة وفي الأنف والحميّة وفي الأخلاق فسُبكوا سبكًا واحدًا وأفرِغوا إفراغًا واحدًا وكان القالب واحدًا[6] تشابهت الأجزاء وتناسب الأخلاط حتّى صار ذلك أشدّ تشابهًا في باب الأعمّ والأخصّ وفي باب الوفاق والمباينة من بعض ذوي الأرحام وجرى عليهم حكم الاتّفاق في الحسب

---

١ كالاختلاف . . . والعربيّ ولا: زيدت من د. ٢ المدريّ والوبريّ: د: المكّيّ والمدنيّ. ٣ د: (وكاختلاف ما بين الطيّ الجبليّ والطيّ السهليّ وكما تقال إنّ هذيلاً أكراد العرب) زيادة. ٤ وبين من نزل الحزان: زيدت من د. ٥ في اللغة . . . على: زيدت من د. ٦ وأفرغوا . . . واحدًا: زيدت من د.

single common origin, have always been very close, and the lands that contain these peoples, even if not exactly corresponding, are substantially alike. In sum, they are all Khurasani, although they each have some distinguishing traits and differ in some respects.

You also contended that the disparity between Turk and Khurasani is not as great as that between Iranian and Arab, Roman and Slav, Zanjī and Ḥabashī, to say nothing of contrasts even more divergent. Rather, the difference between the two is comparable to that between Arabia's town dwellers and tent dwellers,[4] its nomadic and sedentary folk, its residents of the plains and those of the hills. Or it can be compared to the difference between Arabia's lowlanders and uplanders,[5] its inhabitants of valleys and highlands, of lofty plateaus and low-lying tracts. 2.3

You maintained that all these Arabian groups, though they may exhibit differences in language and other characteristics—for we find that the upland clans of Tamīm and the lowland clans of Qays, and the inarticulate speakers of Hawāzin and the eloquent speakers of the Hijaz, are quite distinct in their speech from the Ḥimyarites of the cantons of Yemen; and the same applies to their respective appearances, temperaments, and characters—are all pure Arabs of unadulterated stock, not of mixed race or problematic lineage.[6] Nevertheless, the Turk and the Khurasani do not differ even as much as do Qaḥṭān and ʿAdnān, whose land God has stamped with its set of specific characteristics, just as He has allotted to the people of every region their own distinctive physical form, appearance, character, and language.[7] 2.4

If the question is posed: How can the descendants of Qaḥṭān and ʿAdnān be all Arabs in view of the difference in their ancestry, the answer is that, since the Arabian Peninsula is a unified area, its inhabitants have become assimilated to one norm as regards their native soil, language, temperament, ambition, pride, passion, and manners. They are cast into a single form, and all poured into a single mold, the constituent parts of which are so alike, and its components so harmonious, that, whether one considers broad outline or detail, similarities or dissimilarities, the resultant body is more tightly integrated than are some blood-related groups and is characterized by a consistent ancestral history. 2.5

٦،٢ وصارت هذه الأسباب ولادة أخرى حتّى تناكحوا عليها وتصاهروا من أجلها وامتنعت عدنان قاطبة من مناكحة بني إسحاق وهو أخو إسماعيل وجادوا بذلك في جميع الدهر لبني قحطان وهو ابن عابر[١] ففي إجماع الفريقين على التناكح والتصاهر ومنعهما من ذلك جميع الأمم ككسرى فمن دونه دليل[٢] على أنّ النسب عندهم متّفق وأنّ هذه المعاني قد قامت عندهم مقام الولادة والأرحام الماسّة

٧،٢ وزعمت أنّه أراد الفرقة والتحزيب وأنّك أردت الألفة والتقريب ثمّ زعمت أيضًا أنّ البنويّ خراسانيّ وأنّ نسب الأبناء نسب آبائهم وأنّ حسن صنيع الآباء وقديم فعال الأجداد هو حسب الأبناء وأنّ الموالي بالعرب أشبه وإليهم أقرب وبهم أمسّ لأنّ السنّة قد نقلت الموالي أقرب إلى العرب في كثير من المعاني لأنّهم عرب في المدّعى وفي العاقلة وفي الوراثة وهذا تأويل قوله مولى القوم منهم والولاء لحمة كلحمة النسب

٨،٢ وعلى شبيه ذلك صار حليف القوم منهم وحكمه حكمهم فصار الأخنس بن شريق وهو رجل من ثقيف وكذلك يعلى بن منية وهو رجل من بلعدويّة وكذلك خالد بن عرفطة وهو رجل من عذرة من قريش وبذلك النسب حُرمت الصدقة على موالي بني هاشم فإنّ النبيّ صلّى الله عليه وسلّم أجراهم في باب التنزيه والتطهير مجرى مواليهم وبذلك السبب قدّم النبيّ صلّى الله عليه وسلّم بني عبد المطلّب على بني عبد شمس وقرابتهم سواء ونسبهم واحد للعقد المتقدّم وللأيدي المتّفقة وقال صلّى الله عليه وسلّم منّا خير فارس في العرب عكاشة بن محصن فقال ضرار بن الأزور الأسديّ ذاك رجل منّا يا رسول الله قال بل هو منّا بالحلف فجُعل حليف القوم منهم كما جُعل ابن أخت القوم منهم[٣]

١ وهو ابن عابر: زيدت من د. ٢ ومنعهما . . . دليل: زيدت من د، ق. ٣ وعلى شبيه ذلك . . . القوم منهم: زيدت من د.

These factors constituted for the Arabs an alternative form of genealogical unity to such an extent that they readily intermarried with one other and so have become interrelated. Thus, whereas the ʿAdnān tribes have refrained altogether from intermarrying with the descendants of Isaac, who was Ishmael's brother, they have throughout the ages approved marriage with the tribes descended from Qaḥṭān, who was Eber's son. The agreement of the two groups to intermarry with one another and their refusal to do so with all other peoples, such as Khosrow[8] and lesser figures, is proof that they are in their own eyes a unified race and that accidents of their shared environment have with them replaced real ancestry and close blood relationships. 2.6

You asserted that the other speaker's objective was disharmony and the fostering of factionalism, whereas your aim was harmony and reconciliation. You furthermore declared that the Banawi is a Khurasani, that the clan feeling of sons is the same as that of their fathers, and that the fine deeds of ancestors and the ancient exploits of forebears are a source of pride and honor for their descendants. And you declared that the Mawlas are particularly closely linked to the Arabs, because the law has in many respects put the Mawlas on a similar footing to the Arabs, for they are treated the same as them in the matter of lawsuits, payment of blood money, and inheritance. This is the interpretation of the Prophet's sayings "The Mawla of a tribe is one of them" and "The patron-Mawla relationship is a bond as binding as that of kinship."[9] 2.7

Similarly, a tribe's ally is one of them and judged as belonging to them. Thus, al-Akhnas ibn Shurayq, originally a man of Thaqīf, Yaʿlā ibn Munyah of the Balʿadawiyyah, and Khālid ibn ʿUrfuṭah of ʿUdhrah all came to belong to Quraysh. For the same reason, the Mawlas of the clan of Hāshim were prohibited from sharing in the proceeds of the alms tax, for the Prophet treated them as having the same position as their patrons in their obligation to remain free of contamination and corruption by material gain. Likewise, the Prophet gave precedence to the clan of ʿAbd al-Muṭṭalib over the clan of ʿAbd Shams, although their kinship status within Quraysh was the same and their lineage identical, simply because they had been the first to make alliances with him and offer their consistent support. The Prophet also observed, "To us belongs the best horseman among the Arabs, ʿUkāshah ibn Miḥṣan," whereupon Ḍirār ibn al-Azwar al-Asadī asked, "Is that man one of us, O Messenger of God?" "Certainly," replied Muḥammad, "he is one of us by virtue of alliance, for the ally of a clan is regarded as one of them, just as a sister's son also belongs to that clan." 2.8

٩،٢ ثمّ زعمت أنّ الأتراك قد شاركوا هؤلاء القوم في هذا النسب وصاروا من العرب بهذا السبب مع الذي بانوا به من الخلال وحبوا به من شرف الخصال على أنّ ولاء الأتراك للُباب قريش ولمصاص عبد مناف وفي سرّ هاشم وهاشم موضع العذار من خدّ الفرس ومحلّ العقد من لبّة الكعاب وهم الجوهر المكنون والذهب المصفّى وموضع المحّة من البيضة والعين في الرأس والروح من البدن وهم الأنف المقدّم والسنام الأكوم والطينة البيضاء والدرّة الزهراء والروضة الخضراء والذهب الأحمر فقد شاركوا العرب في أنسابهم وفضلوهم بهذا الفضل الخاصّ الذي لا يبلغه فضل وإن برع بل لا يعشره شرف وإن عظم ولا مجد وإن قدم

١٠،٢ فزعمت أنّ أنساب الجميع متقاربة غير متباعدة وعلى حسب ذلك التقارب تكون الموازرة والمكانفة والطاعة والمناصحة والمحبّة للخلفاء والأئمّة

١،٣ وذكرت أنّه ذكر جملاً من مفاخرة هذه الأجناس وجمهرة من مناقب هذه الأصناف وأنّه جمع ذلك وفصّله وأجمله وفسّره وأنّه ألغى ذكر الأتراك فلم يعرض لهم وأضرب عنهم صفحًا ولم يخبر عنهم كما خبر عن حجّة كلّ جيل وعن برهان كلّ صنف

٢،٣ وذكر أنّ الخراسانيّ يقول نحن النقباء وأبناء النقباء ونحن النجباء وأبناء النجباء ومنّا الدعاة قبل أن تظهر نقابة أو تُعرَف نجابة وقبل المغالبة والمباراة وقبل كشف القناع وزوال التقيّة وبنا زال ملك أعدائنا عن مستقرّه وثبت ملك أوليائنا في نصابه وبيّن ذلك ما قتلنا وشردنا ونهكنا ضربًا وطلبًا وبضعنا بالسيوف الحداد وعذّبنا بألوان العذاب

Then you asserted that the Turks have come to share a close affiliation with this people, and for this reason have become part of the Arabs, along with all the qualities that distinguish them and all the noble characteristics with which they have been endowed. Furthermore, the Turks have a tie of fealty to the very cream of Quraysh, the most excellent of ʿAbd Manāf, the choicest part of Hāshim—and Hāshim is to the rest of Quraysh the cheek strap on the horse's cheek, the necklace on the maiden's bosom, the hidden gem, the refined gold, the yolk to the egg, the eye to the head, the spirit to the body. They are "the aquiline nose, the towering hump,"[10] the white clay,[11] the gleaming pearl, the verdant meadow, the ruddy gold. Thus, the Turks feel at one with their Arab patrons in their sentiments of tribal loyalty, and they even surpass them in this special virtue, which is matched by no other virtue, however eminent, and exceeded by no nobility, however imposing, nor by any glory, however ancient. 2.9

In short, you declared that the relations between all the parts of the caliphal army are convergent, not divergent, and that this convergence gives rise to the support, protection, obedience, sincerity, and love they show to the Rulers. 2.10

The Opponent's Argument for the Disunity of the Army

You mentioned that the other speaker summarized the claims to eminence and excellence of these various groups, presenting that information with detailed and comprehensive explanations. Yet he failed to mention the Turks, paying them no attention whatsoever, and in fact said nothing about them, although he reported the arguments and proofs of every other group. 3.1

The Claims of the Khurasanis

He stated that the Khurasanis said, "We are the leaders of the revolution and sons of the leaders; we are the revolutionary elite and sons of that elite.[12] From among us came the missionaries in the time before the movement's leadership had revealed itself and become known, and before the struggle for supremacy between Umayyads and Abbasids was openly declared and the veil of prudent concealment cast aside. Through us, the dominion of our enemies was cast down from its stronghold and the sovereignty of our patrons was put firmly in its place. During that crisis, we were greatly exposed to death and exile, weakened by blows and thrusts, slashed by swords, and afflicted with every kind of torture. 3.2

٣،٣ وبنا شفى الله تعالى الصدور وأدرك الثأر ومنّا الاثنا عشر النقباء والسبعون النجباء ونحن الخندقيّة وأبناء الخندقيّة ونحن الكفّيّة وأبناء الكفّيّة ومنّا المستجيبة ومن يهرج النيميّة ومنّا نيم خزّان وأصحاب الجوزتين ومنّا الزغنديّة والازادمرديّة ونحن فتحنا البلاد وقتلنا العباد وأبدنا[1] العدوّ بكلّ واد ونحن أصل هذه الدولة ومنبت هذه الشجرة وأصحاب هذه الدعوة ومن عندنا هبّت هذه الريح

٤،٣ الأنصار أنصاران الأوس والخزرج نصروا النبيّ صلّى الله عليه وسلّم في أوّل الزمان وأهل خراسان نصروا ورثته في آخر الزمان غذانا بذلك آباؤنا وغذونا به أبناءنا وصار لنا نسبًا لا نُعرَف إلّا به ودينًا لا نوالي إلّا عليه ثمّ نحن على وتيرة واحدة ومنهاج غير مشترك نُعرَف بالشيعة وندين بالطاعة ونقتل فيها ونموت عليها

٥،٣ سيمانا موصوف ولباسنا معروف ونحن أصحاب الرايات السود والروايات الصحيحة والأحاديث المأثورة والذين يهدمون مدن الجبابرة وينزعون الملك من أيدي الظلمة وفينا تقدّم الخبر وصحّ الأثر وجاء في الحديث صفة الذين يفتحون عمّوريّة ويظهرون عليها ويقتلون مقاتليها ويسبون ذراريّها حيث قالوا في نعتهم شعورهم شعور النساء وثيابهم ثياب الرهبان فصدّق الفعل القول وحقّق الخبر العيان

٦،٣ ونحن الذين ذكرنا وذكر بلاءنا إمام الأئمّة وأبو الخلائف العشرة محمّد ابن عليّ حين أراد توجيه الدعاة إلى الآفاق وتفريق شيعته في البلدان إنّه قال أمّا البصرة وسوادها فقد غلب عليها عثمان وصنائع عثمان فليس بها من شيعتنا إلّا القليل وأمّا الكوفة وسوادها فقد غلب عليها عليّ وشيعة عليّ فليس بها من شيعتنا إلّا القليل وأمّا الشام فشيعة بني مروان وآل أبي سفيان وأمّا الجزيرة فخارجة وحروريّة ومارقة ولكن عليكم بهذا الشرق فإنّ هناك صدورًا سليمة وقلوبًا باسلة لم تفسدها الأهواء ولم تخامرها الأدواء ولم تعتقبها البدع وهم مغيظون موتورون وهناك العدد والعدّة والعتاد والنجدة

---

١ العباد وأبدنا: زيدت من د.

"By our agency, God soothed men's hearts and accomplished His vengeance. From us came the twelve revolutionary leaders and the seventy nobles. We are the warriors of the trenches and the sandy tract,[13] and we are the sons of the same. We are those who respond instantly and are to be trusted in the fray of battle.[14] From us are the faithful of Khazzān and the comrades of al-Jawzatayn.[15] We have the qualities of beasts of prey and of freeborn men.[16] We have conquered all the lands, killed their inhabitants, and destroyed the enemy in every valley. We are the foundation of this dynasty, the soil in which this tree grows, the champions of this cause, and the wind behind its sails. 3.3

"Just as both sections of the Helpers—namely, Aws and Khazraj—helped the Prophet in earlier times, so the Khurasanis have helped his heirs in our day. With this principle our fathers nourished us, and with it we have nourished our sons; it has become for us the only identity by which we are known and the only faith we practice. Furthermore, we have a single code of conduct and a model shared by no other. We are recognized as the partisans of the Prophet's family and our faith is loyalty to that cause; for it we are killed and for it we die. 3.4

"Our standard and our uniform are familiar and recognized. We are the men of black banners, of sound and reliable traditions. We are the ones who demolish the cities of tyrants and wrest sovereignty from the hands of wrongdoers. About us there is an ancient prediction, a saying that has been duly fulfilled, for tradition records the description of those who were to conquer and subdue Amorium, killing its defenders and taking captive its population, saying of their appearance, 'Their hair is women's hair, and their garments are monk's garments.'[17] Surely the event has justified the saying and eyewitness testimony has verified the prediction. 3.5

"We and our heroic deeds have been mentioned by the greatest of the imams, the forefather of the ten caliphs, Muḥammad ibn ʿAlī.[18] When he desired to send missionaries far and wide and spread his activists among the lands, he said, 'Basra and its hinterland is controlled by the devotees of ʿUthmān,[19] and there are few of our partisans there. Kufa and its hinterland is dominated by the party of ʿAlī, and again we have few followers there. Syria is loyal to the sons of Marwān and the descendants of Abū Sufyān, while the Jazīrah is filled with rebels, Ḥarūrīs, and apostates. But look to the east, for there men are to be found of sound bodies and brave hearts, uncorrupted by sectarianism, uninfected by disease, and unimpaired by heresy. They are filled with passion and a thirst for revenge; they are numerous, well prepared, and full of courage.' 3.6

٧،٣ ثمّ قال وأنا أتفاءل إلى حيث ما يطلع منه النهار فكنّا خير جند لخير إمام فصدّقنا ظنّه وثبّتنا رأيه وصوّبنا فراسته وقال مرّة أخرى أمرنا هذا شرقيّ لا غربيّ ومقبل غير مدبر يطلع كطلوع الشمس ويمتدّ على الآفاق امتداد النهار حتّى يبلغ حيث تبلغه الأخفاف وتناله الحوافر

٨،٣ قالوا ونحن قتلنا الصحصحيّة والدالقيّة والذكوانيّة والراشديّة ونحن أصحاب الخنادق أيّام نصر بن سيّار وابن جديع الكرمانيّ وشيبان بن سلمة الخارجيّ ونحن أصحاب[1] نباتة بن حنظلة وعامر بن ضبارة وأصحاب ابن هبيرة فلنا قديم هذا الأمر وحديثه وأوّله وآخره ومنّا قاتل مروان

٩،٣ ونحن قوم لنا أجسام وأجرام وشعور وهام ومناكب عظام وجباه عراض وقصر غلاظ وسواعد طوال ونحن أولد للذكورة وأنسل بعولة وأقلّ ضوى وضؤولة وأقلّ أيامى وأنتق أرحامًا[2] وأشدّ عصبًا وأتمّ عظامًا وأبداننا أحمل للسلاح وتجفافنا أملأ للعيون ونحن أكثر مادّة وأكثر عددًا وعدّة ولو أنّ يأجوج ومأجوج كاثروا من وراء النهر منّا لظهروا عليهم بالعدد فأمّا الأيد وشدّة الأسر فليس لأحد بعد عاد وثمود والعمالقة والكنعانيّين مثل أيدنا وأسرنا ولو أنّ خيول الأرض وفرسان جميع الأطراف جمعوا في حلبة واحدة لكنّا أكثر في العيون وأهول في الصدور

١٠،٣ ومتى رأيت مواكبنا وفرساننا وبنودنا التي لا يحملها غيرنا علمت أنّا لم نُخلق إلّا لقلب الدول وطاعة الخلفاء وتأييد السلطان ولو أنّ أهل التبّت ورجال الزنج وفرسان الهند وحلبة الروم هجم عليهم هاشم بن اشتاخنج لما امتنعوا من طرح السلاح والهرب في البلاد ونحن أصحاب اللحى وأرباب النهى وأهل الحلم والحجى وأهل النجابة في الرأي والبعد من الطيش ولسنا كجند الشام المتعرّضين للحرم والمنتهكين لكلّ محرّم ونحن ناس لنا أمانة وفينا عفّة ونحن نجمع بين النزاهة والقناعة والصبر على الخدمة وعلى التجمير وبعد الشقّة ولنا الطبول المهوّلة والبنود العظام ونحن أصحاب التجافيف والأجراس والبازفكند واللبود الطوال

---

١ أيّام . . . أصحاب: زيدت من د. ٢ وأقلّ إتامًا وأنتق أرحامًا: د: وأجلّ أحسابًا وأوثق أبدانًا.

"Muḥammad ibn ʿAlī further remarked, 'I see a favorable omen in the land whence the day springs. Now we have been the best of troops for the best of imams, and we have justified his opinion, confirmed his view, and vindicated his insight.' On another occasion, he asserted, 'Our policy is centered on the east, not the west; it is forward not backward looking; it will rise like the sun and spread like daylight to the far horizons until it extends as far as the feet of camels and horses can reach.' 3.7

"We killed the Ṣaḥṣaḥiyyah and the Dāliqiyyah, the Dhakwāniyyah and the Rāshidiyyah,[20] and we were the warriors of the trenches in the days of Naṣr ibn Sayyār, Ibn Judayʿ al-Kirmānī, and Shaybān ibn Salamah the Kharijite. We were the men who dealt with Nubātah ibn Ḥanẓalah, ʿĀmir ibn Ḍubārah, and Ibn Hubayrah. From early times until recently, from first to last, we have been the mainstay of this regime. It was one of us who killed the Caliph Marwān. 3.8

"We are a people with mighty frames and fine heads of hair, broad shoulders and wide foreheads, thick necks and long arms. We are unsurpassed in begetting male offspring and producing large families, and few of us are weak-bodied. Our women are seldom widows and their wombs are prolific. We have strong sinews and well-formed bones. Our bodies are perfectly suited for bearing arms, and our horses' armor is the admiration of all. We have abundant supplies, and our numbers and equipment are plentiful. Were the peoples of Gog and Magog to compete in number with those of us who live beyond the River Oxus, our men would surpass them. Nobody, apart from ʿĀd, Thamūd, the Amalekites, and the Canaanites, has the strength and vigor we possess.[21] Were the world's cavalry and its horsemen to be gathered in one arena, we would seem more numerous to onlookers and strike more awe into their hearts. 3.9

"When you see our troops of cavalry and the banners that only we carry, you will realize that we were created for the sole purpose of the overthrow of dynasties, loyalty to the caliphate, and support of the Ruler. Had the infantry of Tibet and East Africa[22] and the cavalries of India and Byzantium faced the onslaught of a Khurasani general such as Hāshim ibn Ishtākhanj, nothing could have restrained them from flinging down their arms and fleeing into the countryside. We are bearded and wise, prudent and discerning, superior in counsel and never reckless. We are not like the Syrian troops, who assail the sanctuary itself[23] and are mired in every vice. We are people who keep faith and exercise self-control and combine purity and moderation. We can bear any kind of service and endure arduous and remote campaigns. We have 3.10

والأغماد المعقّفة والشوارب المعقربة[1] والقلانس الشاشيّة والخيول الشهريّة ولنا الكافركوبات والطبرزينات في الأكفّ والخناجر في الأوساط ولنا تعليق السيوف وحسن الجلسة على ظهور الخيل ولنا الأصوات التي تسقط الحبالى

١١،٣ وليس في الأرض صناعة عراقيّة ولا حجازيّة[2] من أدب وحكمة وحساب وهندسة وارتفاع بناء[3] وصنعة وفقه ورواية نظرت فيها الخراسانيّة إلّا فرعت منها الرؤساء وبذّت فيها العلماء ولنا صنعة السلاح من لبد وركاب ودرع ولنا ممّا جعلناه رياضة وتمرينًا وإرهاصًا[4] عدّة للحرب وتثقيفًا ودربة للمجاولة والمشاولة وللكرّ بعد الفرّ مثل الدبّوق والنزو على الخيل صغارًا ومثل الطبطاب والصوالجة كبارًا ثمّ رمي المجثمّة والبرجاسب والطائر الخاطف فنحن أحقّ بالأثرة وأولى بشرف المنزلة

١٢،٣ قلت وزعم أنّ العربيّ يقول إنّ القربة تستحقّ بالأنساب الثابتة وبالأرحام الشابكة وبالقدمة والطاعة للآباء والعشيرة وبالشكر النافع والمديح الباقي وبالشعر الموزون الذي يبقى بقاء الدهر ويلوح ما لاح نجم وينشد ما أهلّ بالحجّ وما هبّت الصبا وما كان للزيت عاصر وبالكلام المنثور والقول المأثور أو بصفة مخرج الدولة والاحتجاج للدعوة وتقييد المآثر

١٣،٣ إذ لم يكن ذلك من عادة العجم ولا كان حفظ ذلك معروفًا لسوى العرب ونحن نربطها بالشعر المقفّى ونقيّدها بحفظ الأمّيين الذين لا يتّكلون على الكتب المدوّنة والخطوط المطرّسة ونحن أصحاب التفاخر والتنافر والتنازع في الشرف والتحاكم إلى كلّ حكم مقنع وكاهن سجّاع ونحن أصحاب التعاير بالمثالب والتفاخر بالمناقب

١ والشوارب المعقربة: زيدت من د. ٢ عراقيّة ولا حجازيّة: د: عرنبة. ٣ زيدت من ق. ٤ من لبد . . . وإرهاصًا: زيدت من د.

terrifying drums and enormous banners. We boast chain mail, bells, neck scarves,[24] long saddlecloths, curved scabbards, curled mustaches, muslin skullcaps, and sturdy horses. We bear cudgels[25] and double-headed axes in our hands and daggers at our waists. We know how to fasten our swords and how to ride our horses with a good seat, and we can shout so loudly that we make pregnant women miscarry.

"There is no art whatsoever practiced by Iraqis or Hijazis,[26] be it literature or philosophy, mathematics or engineering, construction or manufacturing, law or tradition, in which Khurasanis have not surpassed its experts and outstripped its specialists. We know how to fashion felt-padded armor, stirrups, and coats of mail. We have established training and drills as a foundation and preparation for war and as a means of discipline and practice for maneuvers,[27] such as playing tag and vaulting onto the horse's back for boys, and hockey and polo for men.[28] In addition, we use shooting practice, aiming at fixed and moving targets, and birds in flight.[29] Thus, we deserve to be favorites, worthy of pride of place." 3.11

The Claims of the Arabs

As you remarked, the speaker then asserted that the Arabs said, "The best claim to favor lies in close ties of intermarriage and blood, in ancient ancestry and traditions of loyalty to one's forefathers and clan, and in effective demonstrations of gratitude and enduring expressions of praise. It lies too in that corpus of metrical poetry which will live as long as time, dazzle as long as the stars shine, and be recited as long as the annual pilgrimage is proclaimed or the breeze wafts from the east or the olive is pressed. And you will find it in the scattered reports handed down from of old, in the tale of the dynasty's emergence and the arguments in its favor, and the register of its exploits. 3.12

"For this is not a non-Arab practice: Only the Arabs have been recognized for the preservation of such testimonies—we bind them fast in rhyming verse and confine them to the memory of the unlettered, who do not have to rely on record books or written documents. We are characterized by boastful rivalry and contention for pride of place, and we settle disputes by reference to a competent arbiter or an eloquent[30] diviner. We reproach one another for our failings and boast to one another of our virtues. 3.13

ونحن أحفظ لأنسابنا وأرعى لحقوقنا وتقييدها أيضًا بالمنثور المرسل بعد الموزون المعدّل بلسان أمضى من السنان وأرهف من السيف الحسام حتّى نذكّرهم ما قد درس رسمه وعفا أثره وبين القتال عن الخلفاء من جهة الحميّة ومن طريق العصبيّة[1] وبين القتال من جهة الرغبة والرهبة فرق وليس المعرق في الحفاظ كمن هذا فيه حادث وهذا باب يتقدّم التالد القديم الطارف الحديث وطلّاب الطوائل رجلان سجستانيّ وأعرابيّ ١٤،٣

وهل أكثر النقباء إلّا من صميم العرب ومن صليبة هذا النسب كأبي عبد الحميد قحطبة بن شبيب الطائيّ وأبي محمّد سليمان بن كثير الخزاعيّ وأبي نصر مالك بن الهيثم الخزاعيّ وأبي داود خالد بن إبراهيم الذهليّ وكأبي عمرو لاهز بن قريظ المرئيّ وأبي عيينة موسى بن كعب المرئيّ وأبي سهل القاسم بن مجاشع المرئيّ ومن كان يجري مجرى النقباء ولم يدخل فيهم مثل[2] مالك بن الطوّاف المرئيّ وبعد فمن هذا الذي باشر قتل مروان ومن هزم ابن هبيرة ومن قتل ابن ضبارة ومن قتل نباتة بن حنظلة إلّا عرب الدعوة والصميم من أهل الدولة ومن فتح السند إلّا موسى بن كعب ومن فتح إفريقية إلّا محمّد بن الأشعث ١٥،٣

وقلت وقال ويقول الموالي لنا النصيحة الخالصة والمحبّة الراسخة ونحن موضع الثقة عند الشدّة وعلل المولى من تحت موجبة لمحبّة المولى من فوق لأنّ شرف مولاه راجع إليه وكرمه زائد في كرمه وخموله مسقط لقدره وبودّه أنّ خصال الكرم كلّها اجتمعت فيه لأنّ ذلك كلّما كان مولاه أكبر وأشرف وأظهر كان هو بها أشرف وأنبل ومولاك أسلم لك صدرًا وأودّ ضميرًا وأقلّ حسدًا وبعد فالولاء لحمة كلحمة النسب فقد صار لنا النسب الذي يصوّبه العربيّ ولنا الأصل الذي يفتخر به العجميّ ١٦،٣

[1] وبين . . . العصبيّة: ساقطة من ق. [2] لم ترد في ت، ق.

"We memorize most carefully our genealogies, are most observant of our rights and of recording them also in free-flowing prose and well-balanced verse, in a tongue more penetrating than the spearpoint and sharper than the trenchant sword blade, so that we may remind people of events that have faded away without trace or vestige. To fight for the caliphs out of fervor and solidarity is different from fighting out of desire and fear, and the heir to an ancient tradition of guarding cherished ideals is far superior to one in whom such traditions are new. In this respect, ancient lineage has a great advantage over parvenu stock, and, aside from the men of Sijistān, the Bedouin Arabs have the longest memory for favors and offenses. 3.14

"Were the majority of the leaders of the Abbasid mission not of pure Arab descent?—such as Abū ʿAbd al-Ḥamīd Qaḥṭabah ibn Shabīb al-Ṭāʾī, Abū Muḥammad Sulaymān ibn Kathīr al-Khuzāʿī, Abū Naṣr Mālik ibn al-Haytham al-Khuzāʿī, Abū Dāʾūd Khālid ibn Ibrāhīm al-Dhuhlī, Abū ʿAmr Lāhiz ibn Qurayẓ al-Maraʾī, Abū ʿUyaynah Mūsā ibn Kaʿb al-Maraʾī, Abū Sahl al-Qāsim ibn Mujāshiʿ al-Maraʾī, and men of equal distinction though not numbered among them, such as Mālik ibn al-Ṭawwāf al-Maraʾī and others.[31] Furthermore, who was it who took charge of the assassination of Marwān, who routed Ibn Hubayrah, and who slew Ibn Ḍubārah and Nubātah ibn Ḥanẓalah, if not Arabs of pure stock, devoted to the cause, supporters of the regime? Who but Mūsā ibn Kaʿb conquered Sind; who but Muḥammad ibn al-Ashʿath conquered the Maghrib?" 3.15

The Claims of the Mawlas

You then remarked that he declared that the Mawlas said, "We offer sincere counsel and steadfast affection for the regime and are to be trusted in difficult situations. Indeed, it is the very weakness of the Mawla that ensures his affection for his patron, since the patron's honor reflects well on the Mawla, and the Mawla's reputation increases with that of the patron, whereas ignobility on the part of the patron diminishes the status of the Mawla. The Mawla therefore takes delight in having all possible qualities of nobility combined in his patron, because the greater, nobler, and more distinguished the patron is, the more honored and ennobled the Mawla is too. Consequently, your Mawla is the most well-disposed and congenial toward you and the least inclined to envy. Furthermore, they say there is no attachment so strong as the attachment of clan affiliation, and we have both the clan affiliation approved by the Arab and the ethnic origin acclaimed by the non-Arab. 3.16

قال والصبر ضروب فأكرمها كلّها الصبر على إفشاء السرّ وللمولى في هذه المكرمة ما ليس لأحد ونحن أخصّ مدخلاً وألطف في الخدمة مسلكًا ولنا مع الطاعة والخدمة والإخلاص وحسن النيّة خدمة الأبناء للآباء والآباء للأجداد ١٧،٣

وهم بمواليهم آنس وبناحيتهم أوثق وبكفايتهم أسرّ وقد كان المنصور ومحمّد بن عليّ وعليّ بن عبد الله يخصّون مواليهم بالمواكلة والبسط والإيناس لا يبهرجون الأسود لسواده ولا الدميم لدمامته ولا الصناعة الدنيئة لدناءتها ويوصون بحفظهم أكابر أولادهم ويجعلون لكثير من موتاهم الصلاة على جنائزهم وذلك بحضرة من العمومة وبني الأعمام والأخوة ١٨،٣

ويتذاكرون إكرام رسول الله صلّى الله عليه وسلّم لزيد بن حارثة مولاه حين عقد له يوم مؤتة على جلّة بني هاشم وجعله أمير كلّ بلدة يطؤها ويتذاكرون حبّه لأسامة بن زيد وهو الحبّ ابن الحبّ وعقد له على عظماء المهاجرين وأكابر الأنصار ويتذاكرون صنيعه بسائر مواليه كأبي أنسة وشقران وفلان وفلان ١٩،٣

قالوا ولنا صاحب الدولة أبو مسلم عبد الرحمن بن مسلم وأبو سلمة حفص بن سليمان وأبو مسلم مولى الإمام وعليهما دارت رحى الدولة وتمّ الأمر واتّسق نظام الملك قالوا ولنا من رؤوس النقباء أبو منصور مولى خزاعة وأبو حكم عيسى بن أعين مولى خزاعة[١] وأبو الحمزة عمرو بن أعين مولى خزاعة وأبو النجم عمران بن إسماعيل مولى آل أبي معيط ٢٠،٣

فلنا مناقب الخراسانيّة ولنا مناقب الموالي في هذه الدعوة ونحن منهم وإليهم ومن أنفسهم لا يدفع ذلك مسلم ولا ينكره مؤمن خدمناهم كبارًا وحملناهم على ٢١،٣

---

١ أبو حكم . . . خزاعة: زيدت من ق.

"There are several kinds of self-control, but the noblest is refraining from 3.17
divulging a secret, and to this virtue the Mawla has a better claim than anyone. Our behavior is the most refined, and our service is most courteously conducted. In addition to loyalty, we espouse attentiveness, sincerity, and good intentions, the sort of devotion a son feels for his father, or that of a father for his own father.

"For their part, our Arab patrons are most kind to their Mawlas, with 3.18
absolute confidence in their intentions and delight in their competence. Al-Manṣūr, Muḥammad ibn ʿAlī, and ʿAlī ibn ʿAbdallāh all used to display toward their Mawlas a particular degree of mutual confidence, openness, and geniality. They did not disregard the black person because of his blackness or the ugly person because of his foul appearance or the practitioner of a humble trade because of his lowliness. In their wills, they would entrust their Mawlas to the care of their eldest sons. In many cases, when Mawlas died, the patrons performed the prayer over their biers, and that even in the presence of uncles, cousins,[32] or brothers of the deceased.

"In conversation, they would recall how the Prophet honored his Mawla, 3.19
Zayd ibn Ḥārithah, when he appointed him at the Battle of Mu'tah to the command over the cream of the Hashimites and nominated him governor of any town he might subdue. They would recall the love shown by the Prophet for Usāmah ibn Zayd, who succeeded his father as the Prophet's favorite, for he gave him command over the principal leaders of both Emigrants and Helpers. And they would recollect his favor toward his other Mawlas, such as Abū Anasah, Shaqrān, and many more like them.

"Ours too, they say, is that champion of the Abbasid dynastic cause, 3.20
Abū Muslim ʿAbd al-Raḥmān ibn Muslim, and also Abū Salamah Ḥafṣ ibn Sulaymān. Abū Muslim was the imam's own Mawla, and both men were key to the regime's revolutionary policy, to its achievement of power, and to the smooth running of its administration. To us, they say, belong, among the chief Abbasid leaders, Abū Manṣūr, Abū l-Ḥakam ʿĪsā ibn Aʿyan, and Abū Ḥamzah ʿAmr ibn Aʿyan, all three being Mawlas of the tribe of Khuzāʿah, and Abū Najm, Mawla of the clan of Abū l-Muʿayṭ.[33]

"In this political cause, we Mawlas possess the same virtues as the Khurasa- 3.21
nis, as well as our own personal virtues. We belong to the Abbasids and stand as one with them; this no true Muslim can possibly deny. We served them when they were adults and carried them on our shoulders when they were

عواتقنا صغارًا هذا مع حقّ الرضاع والخؤولة والنشوء في الكتّاب والتقلّب في تلك العراص التي لم يبلغها إلّا كلّ سعيد الجدّ وجيه في الملوك

٢٢،٣ فقد شاركنا العربيّ في فخره والخراسانيّ في مجده والبنويّ في فضله ثمّ تفرّدنا بما لم يشاركونا فيه ولا سابقونا إليه قالوا ونحن أشكل بالرعيّة وأقرب إلى طباع الدهماء وهم بنا آنس وإلينا أسكن وإلى لقائنا أحنّ ونحن بهم أرحم وعليهم أعطف وبهم أشبه فمن أحقّ بالأثرة وأولى بحسن المنزلة ممّن هذه الخصال له وهذه الخلال فيه

٢٣،٣ وقلت وذكرت أنّ البنويّ قال نحن أصل خراسانيّ وهي مخرج الدولة ومطلع الدعوة ومنها نجم هذا القرن وصبأ هذا الناب وتفجّر هذا الينبوع واستفاض هذا البحر حتّى ضرب الحقّ بجرانه وطبّق الآفاق بضيائه فأبرأ من السقم القديم[١] وشفى من الداء العضال وأغنى من العيلة وبصّر من العمى وفرعي بغداد وهي مستقرّ الخلافة والقرار بعد الحولة وفيها بقيّة رجال الدعوة وأبناء أبناء الشيعة وهي خراسان العراق وبيت الخلافة وموضع المادّة

٢٤،٣ قال وأنا أعرق في هذا الأمر من أبي وأكثر تردادًا فيه من جدّي وأحقّ في هذا الفضل من المولى والعربيّ ولنا بعد في انفسنا ما لا ينكر من الصبر تحت ظلال السيوف القصار والرماح الطوال ولنا معانقة الأبطال عند تحطّم القنا وانقطاع الصفائح ولنا المواجأة بالسكاكين وتلقّي الخناجر بالعيون ونحن حماة المستلحم وأبناء المضايق ونحن أهل الثبات عند الجولة والمعرفة عند الحيرة وأصحاب المشهّرات وزينة العساكر وحليّ الجيوش ومن يمشي في الرمح ويختال بين الصفّين ونحن أصحاب الفتك والإقدام

---

١ زيدت من ق.

infants. Furthermore, we are tied to them by the bonds of common foster parentage, by our daughters becoming their wives,[34] by sharing the same schooling, and by moving in those ample courtyards to which none have access save men favored by good fortune and distinguished by high rank.

"We can share with the Arab in his pride, with the Khurasani in his glory, and with the Banawi in his excellence. Yet we have one quality they do not share with us and in which they do not rival us. For we, they say, have an affinity with the common folk, and are in touch with the sentiments of the populace, who are friendly with us, at ease in our company, and keen to mingle with us, since we are particularly sympathetic and well-disposed toward them and share the same outlook. Who, therefore, is more deserving of preference and more entitled to high status than those who possess such qualities and characteristics?" 3.22

The Claims of the Banawis

Then he said, as you recounted, that the Banawis said, "Our roots are in Khurasan, which is the place where the regime started, where the dynastic cause had its origins. From there this horn sprouted, this fang broke through, this spring gushed, and this sea swelled, until the right way was established, encompassing the far horizons in its luster, curing long-seated sickness and chronic disease, bringing wealth in place of destitution and sight instead of blindness. However, our present base is Baghdad, which is the permanent seat of the caliphate and a place of stability after change. Here are to be found the offspring of the regime's missionaries and the descendants of the revolution's founders. It is the Khurasan of Iraq, home of the caliphate, and the place where it is nourished. 3.23

"I am more deeply committed to the regime than my father and more devoted to it than my grandfather, and worthier of this claim of excellence than the Mawla or the Arab. Moreover, we undeniably show endurance when exposed to short swords or long lances. We wrestle with heroic warriors when spears clash and sword blades are shattered, and we thrust with knives and engage with daggers at close quarters. We are defenders of those hard pressed in battle and are accustomed to desperate situations. We are men of constancy amid flux, of clear understanding amid confusion. We are soldiers of high repute, the brightest jewels in the army. We are men who march forward into the thick of oncoming lances and stride proudly between the battle lines, masters of the lethal assault and the relentless advance. 3.24

ولنا بُعد التسلّق ونقب المدن والتقحّم على ظبات السيوف وأطراف الرماح ورضخ الجندل وهشم العمد والصبر على الجراح وعلى جرّ السلاح إذا طار قلب الأعرابيّ وساء ظنّ الخراسانيّ ثمّ الصبر تحت العقوبة والاحتجاج عند المساءلة واجتماع العقل وصحّة الطرف وثبات القدمين وقلّة التكفّي بحبل العقابين والبعد من الإقرار وقلّة الخضوع للدهر والخضوع عند جفوة الزوّار وجفاء الأقارب والإخوان ولنا القتال عند أبواب الخنادق ورؤوس القناطر ونحن الموت الأحمر عند أبواب النقب ولنا المواجأة في الأزقّة والصبر على قتال السجون فسل عن ذلك الخليديّة والكتيفيّة والبلاليّة والخريبيّة ٢٥٫٣

ونحن أصحاب المكابرات وأرباب البيات وقتل الناس جهارًا في الأسواق والطرقات ونحن نجمع بين السلّة والمزاحفة وبين القنا الطوال ما كنّا رجالة والمطارد القصار ما كنّا فرسانًا فإن صرنا كمنًا فالحتف القاضي والسمّ الذعاف وإن كنّا طلائع فكلّنا يقوم مقام أمير الجيش نقاتل بالليل كما نقاتل بالنهار ونقاتل في الماء كما نقاتل على الأرض ونقاتل في القرية كما نقاتل في المحلّة ونحن أفتك وأخبث ونحن أقطع للطريق وأذكر في الثغور مع حسن القدود وجودة الخرط ومقادير اللحى وحسن العمّة والنفس المرّة ٢٦٫٣

وأصحاب البطالة[1] والفتوّة ثمّ الخطّ والكتابة والفقه والرواية ولنا بغداد بأسرها تسكن ما سكنّا وتتحرّك ما تحرّكنا والدنيا كلّها معلّقة بها وصائرة إلى معناها فإذا كان هذا أمرها وقدرها فجميع الدنيا تبع لها وكذلك أهلها لأهلها وفتّاكها لفتّاكها وخلّاعها لخلّاعها ورؤساؤها لرؤسائها وصلحاؤها لصلحائها ونحن تربية الخلفاء وجيران الوزراء ولدنا في أفنية ملوكنا ونحن أجنحة خلفائنا فأخذنا بآدابهم واحتذينا على مثالهم فلسنا نعرف سواهم ولا نهتمّ بغيرهم ولا يطمع فينا أحد قطّ من خطّاب ملكهم وممّن يترشّح للاعتراض عليهم فمن أحقّ بالأثرة وأولى بالقرب في المنزلة ممّن هذه الخصال فيه وهذه الخلال له ٢٧٫٣

١ ت، ق: الباطل.

"Furthermore, we scale and breach city walls, charge headlong at the blades of swords and points of lances, crush the enemy like a rock and smash them like pillars. We endure injury and the strain of hauling weapons when the Bedouin Arab would lose heart and the Khurasani would despair. We can bear torture and hold our own under interrogation, keeping our minds focused, our gaze unflinching, our stance unyielding. Seldom does whipping us at the stake suffice to break us, and the chance of obtaining a confession from us is remote. Rarely do we yield to fate or submit when mistreated by newcomers and scorned by kinsmen and brothers. We do battle in the narrow confines of ditches and on the tops of bridges, and we storm the breaches like wild animals. We engage in hand-to-hand street fighting and excel at close combat. Just ask the Khālidiyyah, the Katīfiyyah, the Bilāliyyah, and the Khuraybiyyah.[35] 3.25

"We are masters of resistance tactics and of night assaults, and of brazen daylight killings in marketplace and street. We are equally at home in a cavalry charge and a slow march, in wielding long lances as infantrymen and short stabbing spears on horseback. In an ambush, we are like a death knell, a deadly poison, and in a vanguard detachment, every one of us is as good as a general. We fight equally well by night or day, on water or land, in the country village or the city quarter. We are extremely deadly and violent, highly effective in barring a road, and very vigilant on a frontier. We have a handsome physique, a fine shape, well-proportioned beards, beautiful turbans, and a valiant spirit. 3.26

"We are men of bravery and chivalry, yet we are also masters in calligraphy and composition, law and tradition. All of Baghdad is ours: It is tranquil so long as we are calm but in turmoil if we are roused. All the world depends on it and adapts itself to Baghdad's outlook. Because of its status and power, the rest of the world is subordinate to it. Everyone else follows the lead of its inhabitants, whether one considers violent criminals and debauchees or nobles and honest men. Furthermore, we are the tutors of caliphs and the neighbors of viziers; we are born in the palace grounds of our leaders and are the protective wings of our caliphs. We have adopted their ways, and we follow their example; we acknowledge only them and take no interest in anyone else. No hope of winning us over has ever been entertained by any pretender to their sovereignty or by anyone proposing to challenge their authority. Who, therefore, is more deserving of preference and more entitled to proximity in status to the caliphs than those who possess these qualities and characteristics?" 3.27

إن ذهبنا حفظك الله بعقب هذه الاحتجاجات وعند مقطع هذه الاستدلالات نستعمل المفاوضة بمناقب الأتراك والمقاربة بين خصالهم وخصال كلّ صنف من هذه الأصناف سلكنا في هذا الكتاب سبيل أصحاب الخصومات في كتبهم وطريق أصحاب الأهواء في الاختلاف الذي بينهم وكتابنا هذا إنّما تكلّفناه لنؤلّف بين قلوبهم إن كانت مختلفة ولنزيد في الألفة إن كانت مؤتلفة ولنخبر عن اتّفاق أسبابهم لتجتمع كلمتهم ولتسلم صدورهم وليعرف من كان لا يعرف منهم موضع التفاوت في النسب وكم مقدار الخلاف في الحسب لئلّا يغيّر بعضهم مغيّر ويفسده عدوّ بأباطيل مموّهة وشبهات مزوّرة فإنّ المنافق العليم والعدوّ ذا الكيد العظيم قد يصوّر لمن دونه الباطل في صورة الحقّ ويلبس الإضاعة ثياب الحزم ١،٤

إلّا أنّا على حال سنذكر جملاً من أحاديث رويناها وأمورًا رأيناها وشاهدناها وقصصًا تلقّفناها من أفواه الحكماء وسمعناها وسنذكر ما حُفظ في جميع الأصناف من الآلات والأدوات ثمّ ننظر أيّهم لها أشدّ استعمالاً وبها أشدّ استقلالاً ومن أثقب حسبًا وأيقظ عينًا وأذكى نفسًا وأشدّ غورًا وأجمع أمرًا[1] وأعمّ خواطر وأكثر غرائب وأبدع طريقًا[2] وأكثر نفعًا في الحروب وضرًّا[3] وأدرب دربة وأغمض مكيدة وأشدّ احتراسًا وألطف احتيالاً حتّى يكون الخيار في يد الناظر في هذا الكتاب المتصفّح لمعانيه والمقلّب لوجوهه والمفكّر في أبوابه والمقابل بين أوّله وآخره ٢،٤

١ وأجمع أمرًا: زيدت من د. ٢ وأكثر . . . . طريقًا: زيدت من د. ٣ وأكثر نفعًا . . . وضرًّا: د: وأدوم نفعًا في الحروب وأضرى.

Part II

The Aims and Theoretical Basis of al-Jāḥiẓ's Response

If we proceed, may God preserve you, on the basis of what follows from these arguments and in line with where these conclusions lead, embarking on a discussion of the virtues of the Turks and a comparison between their qualities and those of each of the other categories, we will be treading the same path in our treatise as polemicists do in their writings, following in the way of partisan thinkers in their disputes among themselves. However, we have only undertaken this work to reconcile hearts where they are discordant, to increase such mutual understanding as already exists, and to ascertain the essential unity of the various positions so that their opinions may be reconciled and their minds set at rest. Furthermore, it may be made clear to those who are ignorant of such things what the true significance is of variation in group membership and of differences in social standing lest some devious enemy muddle or mislead them with specious falsehoods and fake sophisms. For a clever dissembler or a cunning opponent can easily present to an ignorant person falsehood in the shape of truth and dress up prodigality in the guise of prudence. 4.1

In any case, we shall record a number of anecdotes that have been recounted to us and some matters we have witnessed personally, as well as stories we have picked up and heard from the mouths of informed persons. We shall describe the talents and abilities[36] that each of the groups under discussion here preserves, investigating which of them deploys them to best effect or has the exclusive possession of them. Then we will examine which of them has the most penetrating and perspicacious powers of reckoning, the brightest and deepest intellect, the most wide-ranging and expansive ideas, the most creative and innovative approach; which has been the most effective in inflicting damage in war, with the best training and most impenetrable stratagems; and which is the most prudent and can find the smartest way out of difficulties. The final assessment will rest with the readers of this treatise, those who study its ideas, turn over in their minds the points it makes, ponder its contents, and check it through from beginning to end. We ourselves have no intention of taking sides 4.2

ولا نكون نحن انتحلنا شيئًا دون شيء وتقلّدنا تفضيل بعض على بعض بل لعلّنا أن لا نخبر عن خاصّة ما عندنا بحرف واحد فإذا دبّرنا كتابنا هذا التدبير وكان موضوعًا على هذه الصفة كان أبعد له من مذاهب الجدال والمراء واستعمال الهوى

٣،٤ وقد ظنّ ناس كثير أنّ أسماء أصناف الأجناد لمّا اختلفت في الصورة والخطّ والهجاء أنّ حقائقها ومعانيها على حسب ذلك وليس الأمر على ما يتوهّمون ألا ترى أنّ اسم الشاكريّة وإن خالف في الصورة والخطّ والهجاء اسم الجند فإنّ المعنى فيهما ليس ببعيد لأنّهم يرجعون إلى معنى واحد وعلم واحد والذي يرجعون إليه طاعة الخلفاء وتأييد السلطان

٤،٤ وإذا كان المولى منقولاً إلى العرب في أكثر المعاني ومجعولاً منهم في عامّة الأسباب لم يكن ذلك بأعجب من جعل الخال والدًا والحليف من الصميم وابن الأخت من القوم وقد جعل الله ابن الملاعنة المولود على فراش البعل منسوبًا إلى أمّه

٥،٤ وقد جعل إسماعيل وهو ابن أعجميّين عربيًا لأنّ الله تعالى لمّا فتق لهاته بالعربيّة المبينة على غير التلقين والترتيب وفطره على الفصاحة العجيبة على غير النشوء والتمرين وسلخ طباعه من طبائع العجم ونقل إلى بدنه تلك الأجزاء وركّبه اختراعًا على ذلك التركيب وسوّاه تلك التسوية وصاغه تلك الصياغة ثمّ حباه من طبائعهم ومنحه من أخلاقهم وشمائلهم وطبعه من كرمهم وأنفتهم وهممهم على أكرمها وأسناها وأشرفها وأعلاها وجعل ذلك برهانًا على رسالته ودليلاً على نبوّته وصار أحقّ بذلك النسب وأولى بشرف ذلك الحسب

٦،٤ وكما جُعل إبراهيم أبًا لمن لم يلد فالبنويّ خراسانيّ من جهة الولادة والمولى عربيّ من جهة المدّعي والعاقلة ولو أحاط علمنا بأنّ زيدًا لم يُخلَق من نجل عمرو إلّا عهارًا لنفيناه عنه[١] وإن أيقنّا أنّه لم يُخلَق إلّا من ماء صلبه وكما جعل النبيّ أزواجه

---

١ عهارًا لنفيناه عنه: د: بما هو ألحقناه به.

one way or another, nor of assuming the responsibility for expressing preference for one over another. Rather, we hope not to utter a single word expressive of our own opinion. If we design and set down our treatise in this way, then it will avoid any aspect of contentious debate or prejudicial treatment.

Many people have thought that since the names of the various types of troops differ in form, writing, and spelling, the underlying realities and meanings are similarly different. But the matter is not as they suppose. Although the term "personal guard" differs in form, writing, and spelling from the word "army regiment,"[37] it is obvious that the meaning of the two is very little differentiated, for they are both reducible to the same basic idea—namely, loyalty to the caliph and support for the government. 4.3

If the Mawlas can be assigned to the same position as the Arabs for most purposes and be reckoned as one of them in most situations, that is in no way more surprising than treating a maternal uncle as a father, or an ally as belonging to the main body of a tribe, or a sister's son as one of the family. And in the case of a son repudiated by his father due to suspicion of the mother's adultery, God has allowed that he be attributed to the maternal line. 4.4

Ishmael, though born of two non-Arab parents, was counted an Arab because God gave his throat the facility of[38] speaking clear Arabic, though he had received no teaching or instruction, and then endowed him with wondrous eloquence, though he had not been brought up in it or received any training. He also divested him of the non-Arab stamp in his nature, transplanted new features into his body, and by a creative act reconstructed him in that new form, smoothing and shaping him afresh. Then He endowed him with the attributes of the Arabs, gave him their temperament and character, and stamped him with their nobility, pride, and ambition to the greatest possible extent. He did this as proof of Ishmael's divine mission and status as a prophet, and thus he became most deserving of that ancestry and most worthy of the honor of such noble qualities.[39] 4.5

Just as Abraham was made a father of those whom he did not beget, so the Banawi is a Khurasani by descent, and the Mawla is an Arab for legal purposes.[40] Similarly, suppose that we were aware that Zayd was only the son of ʿAmr by adultery—we would refuse to acknowledge ʿAmr's paternity, however certain we were that Zayd was the fruit of ʿAmr's loins.[41] In like manner, the Prophet considered his wives to be mothers of the believers even though they did not bear or suckle them, and some readings of the sacred text add to «His wives 4.6

أمّهات المؤمنين وهنّ لم يلدنهم ولا أرضعنهم وفي بعض القراءات ﴿وَأَزْوَاجُهُ أُمَّهَاتُهُمْ﴾ وَهُوَ أَبٌ لَهُمْ على قوله ﴿مِلَّةَ أَبِيكُمْ إِبْرَاهِيمَ﴾

٧،٤ وجعل المرأة من جهة الرضاع أمًّا وجعل امرأة البعل أمّ ولد البعل من غيرها وجعل الرأب والدًا وجعل العمّ في كتاب الله أبًا وهم عبيده لا يتقلّبون إلّا فيما قلّبهم فيه وله أن يجعل من عباده من شاء عربيًّا ومن شاء أعجميًّا ومن شاء قرشيًّا ومن شاء زنجيًّا كما له أن يجعل من شاء ذكرًا ومن شاء أنثى ومن شاء خنثى ومن شاء أخرجه من ذلك فجعله لا ذكرًا ولا أنثى ولا خنثى

٨،٤ وكذلك خلق الملائكة وهم أكرم على الله من جميع الخليقة فلم يجعل لآدم أبًا ولا أمًّا وخلقه من طين ونسبه إليه وخلق حوّاء من ضلع آدم وجعلها له زوجًا وسكنًا وخلق عيسى من غير ذكر ونسبه إلى أمّه التي خلقه منها وخلق الجانّ من نار السموم وآدم من طين وعيسى من غير نطفة وخلق السماء من دخان والأرض من الماء وخلق إسحاق من عاقر وأنطق عيسى في المهد وأنطق يحيى بالحكمة وهو صبيّ وعلّم سليمان منطق الطير وكلام النمل وعلّم الحفظة من الملائكة جميع الألسنة حتّى كتبوا بكلّ خطّ ونطقوا بكلّ لسان وأنطق ذئب أهبان بن أوس

٩،٤ والمؤمنون من جميع الأمم إذا دخلوا الجنّة وكذلك أطفالهم والمجانين منهم يتكلّمون ساعة يدخلون الجنّة بكلام أهل الجنّة على غير الترتيب والتنزيل والتعليم على طول الأيّام والتلقين فكيف يتعجّب الجاهلون من إنطاق إسماعيل بالعربيّة على غير تعليم الآباء وتأديب الحواضن وهذه المسألة ربّما سأل عنها بعض القحطانيّة ممّن لا علم له لبعض العدنانيّة وهي على حال القحطانيّة أشدّ فأمّا جواب العدنانيّ فسلس النظام سهل المخرج قريب المعنى لأنّ بني قحطان لا يدّعون لقحطان نبوّة فيعطيه الله تعالى مثل هذه الأعجوبة

١٠،٤ وما الذي قسم الله بين الناس من ذلك إلّا كما صنع في طينة الأرض فجعل بعضها حجرًا وبعض الحجر ياقوتًا وبعضه ذهبًا وبعضه نحاسًا وبعضه رصاصًا وبعضه صفرًا وبعضه حديدًا وبعضه ترابًا وبعضه فخارًا وكذلك الزاج والمغرة

are their mothers» the words "and he is a father to them," conforming to God's statements about «the religion of Abraham your father».[42]

Similarly, a woman is treated as a mother by virtue of having suckled an infant, as is a wife who acts as mother to her husband's children by another woman; also, the man who brings up a child is regarded as a father to it, as is the uncle, according to the Qur'an.[43] All these are God's subjects and take whatever form He has ordained for them. It is within His power to make whichever of His servants He wishes into an Arab or a non-Arab, a Qurashī or a Zanjī. Similarly, He can make whomsoever He pleases a male or a female, a hermaphrodite, or something else entirely. 4.7

So, too, He created the angels, who are nobler in His sight than all the rest of Creation. He did not appoint for Adam a father or a mother, but created him from clay, which was his origin. He created Eve from Adam's rib and made her a wife and a comfort to him. He created Jesus without a male parent and assigned him to the mother from whom He had been created. He created the jinn from scorching fire, Adam from clay, and Jesus without the seed of man. He created the heavens from smoke and the earth from water, and Isaac from a barren woman. He caused Jesus to speak in the cradle and John the Baptist to utter wisdom while still a child. He taught Solomon the language of the birds and the speech of the ants. He taught the recording angels all tongues so they could write in every script and speak in every tongue, and He gave the faculty of speech to the wolf of Uhbān ibn Aws. 4.8

When the believers of all nations enter paradise, including children and fools, they will at once speak the language of the inhabitants of paradise, without preparation, inspiration, lengthy teaching, or instruction. Why then are the unlearned astonished at Ishmael being made to speak Arabic without the teaching of his forebears or training of his nurses? This question may well have been put by an uninformed Qaḥṭānī to an ʿAdnānī, for the problem is more awkward for a Qaḥṭānī. The ʿAdnānī's answer is simple and easy to formulate, and it makes good sense,[44] but the Qaḥṭānī cannot claim any prophetic status for their ancestor Qaḥṭān such as would oblige God to give him the same miraculous power as He gave to Ishmael. 4.9

The divisions God has made among men are no different from those He has made in the composition of the earth. Part of it He has made into minerals—for example, ruby, gold, copper, lead, brass, and iron—and part soil and clay, as well as vitriol, red ochre, arsenic, galena, sulfur, tar, zinc, ammonia, 4.10

والزرنيخ والمرتك والكبريت والقار والتوتيا والنوشادر والمرقشيثا والمغناطيس ومن يحصي عدد جواهر الأرض وأصناف الفلز وإذا كان الأمر على ما وصفنا فالبنويّ خراسانيّ وإذا كان الخراسانيّ مولى والمولى عربيّ فقد صار الخراسانيّ والبنويّ والمولى والعرب شيئًا واحدًا وأدنى ذلك أن يكون الذي معهم من خصال الوفاق غامرًا لما معهم من خصال الخلاف بل هم في معظم الأمر وفي كبر الشأن وعمود النسب متّفقون فالأتراك خراسانيّة وموالي الخلفاء قصرة فقد صار فضل التركيّ إلى الجميع راجعًا وصار شرفهم زائدًا في شرفهم

١١،٤ وإذا عرف سائر الأجناد ذلك سامحت النفوس وذهب التعقيد ومات الضغن وانقطع سبب الاستثقال فلم يبق إلّا التحاسد والتنافس الذي لا يزال يكون بين المتقاربين في القرابة وفي الصناعة وفي المجاورة على أنّ التوازر والتسالم في القرابات وفي بني الأعمام والعشائر أفشى وأعمّ من التخاذل والتعادي[1] ولحبّ التناصر والحاجة إلى التعاون انضمّ بعض القبائل في البوادي إلى بعض ينزلون معًا ويظعنون معًا

١٢،٤ ومن فارق أصحابه أقلّ ومن نصر ابن عمّه أكثر ومن اغتبط بنعمته وتمنّى بقاءها والزيادة فيها أكثر ممّن بغاها الغوائل وتمنّى انقطاعها وزوالها ولا بدّ في أضعاف ذلك من بعض التنافس والتخاذل إلّا أنّ ذلك قليل من كثير وليس يكون أن تصفو الدنيا وتنقى من الفساد والمكروه حتّى يموت جميع الخلاف وتستوي لأهلها وتتمهّد لسكّانها على ما يشتهون ويهوون لأنّ ذلك من صفة دار الجزاء وليس كذلك صفة دار العمل

١٣،٤ هذا كتاب كتبته أيّام المعتصم بالله رضي الله عنه ونضّر وجهه فلم يصل إليه لأسباب يطول ذكرها فلذلك لم أعرض للإخبار عنها وأحببت أن يكون كتابًا قصدًا ومذهبًا عدلًا ولا يكون كتاب إسراف في مديح قوم وإغراق في هجاء آخرين فإنّ الكتاب إذا كان كذلك شابه الكذب[2] وخالطه التزيّد وبُني أساسه على التكلّف

١ التخاذل والتعادي: د: البعداء وتخوّف التخاذل. ٢ زيدت من د.

marcasite, and magnesium. But who can enumerate all the elements in the earth and the various types of ore? If matters are as we say—namely, that the earth, though one, comprises numerous elements—then we may conclude that, similarly, the Banawi is a Khurasani, and since the Khurasani is a Mawla and the Mawla is an Arab by adoption, the Khurasani, Banawi, Mawla, and Arab are all identical in essence. Or, to put it more exactly, the qualities they have in common predominate over those in which they differ. In fact, they are largely homogenous as regards status and affiliation. Likewise, the Turks are on par with the Khurasanis and the Mawlas of the caliphs. The virtues of the Turk redound to the credit of all the rest, and his honor increases theirs.

If all the troops realized this, their inflamed tempers would subside, quarrels and grudges would fade away, and the grounds for recrimination would be removed. There would only remain such mutual rivalry and competitiveness as is constantly to be found among those thrown together by kinship, occupation, or neighborhood. Nevertheless, mutual assistance and friendly feeling are more widespread and general among kinfolk, cousins, and tribal groups than dissension and enmity. It is because of the desire for mutual support and the need for cooperation that the tribes of the desert attach themselves to one another, encamping and migrating together. 4.11

Those who abandon their comrades are few, and it is very common for a man to help his cousin. A man delights in his cousin's prosperity and wishes it to continue and increase far more often than he longs for disaster to overtake it or hopes for it to come to an end. Of course, there is a certain amount of rivalry and dissension mixed up with all this, but this is comparatively rare. It is not feasible that the world should be pure and unsullied by any corruption or evil so that all differences should fade away, nor that the world be entirely even and equal for its inhabitants in a way they might yearn for, since that is a quality of paradise, not of this workaday life. 4.12

I originally wrote this essay in the time of al-Muʿtaṣim, may God be pleased with him and keep him in splendor, but it was not communicated to him for reasons that would take too long to recount and that I therefore refrain from stating. I wished it to be a text moderate in tone and fair in attitude, not extravagant in the praise of one group and excessive in the abuse of others. A treatise of the latter sort is marred by falsehood and tainted by extremism; 4.13

وخرج كلامه مخرج الاستكراه والتعليق وأنفع المدائح للمادح وأجداها على الممدوح وأبقاها أثرًا وأحسنها ذكرًا أن يكون المديح صدقًا ولظاهر حال الممدوح موافقًا وبه لائقًا حتّى لا يكون من المعبّر عنه والواصف له إلّا الإشارة إليه والتنبيه عليه

١٤،٤ وأنا أقول إن كان لا يمكن ذكر مناقب الأتراك إلّا بذكر مثالب سائر الأجناد فترك ذكر الجميع أصوب والإضراب عن هذا الكتاب أحزم وذكر الكثير من هذه الأصناف بالجميل لا يقوم إلّا بالقليل من ذكر بعضهم بالقبيح لأنّ ذكر الأكثر بالجميل نافلة وباب من التطوّع وذكر الأقلّ بالقبيح معصية وباب من ترك الواجب وقليل الفريضة أجدى علينا من كثير التطوّع ولكلّ الناس نصيب من النقص ومقدار من الذنوب وإنّما يتفاضل بكثرة المحاسن وقلّة المساوي فأمّا الاشتمال على جميع المحاسن والسلامة من جميع المساوي دقيقها وجليلها وظاهرها وخفيها فهذا ما يعرفونه فيهم

١٥،٤ وقد قال النابغة

وَلَسْتَ بِمُسْتَبْقٍ أَخًا لا تَلُمُّهُ عَلَى شَعَثٍ أَيُّ ٱلرِّجَالِ ٱلْمُهَذَّبُ

١٦،٤ وقال حريش السعديّ

أَخٌ لِي كَأَيَّامِ ٱلْحَيَاةِ إِخَاؤُهُ تَلَوَّنُ أَلْوَانًا عَلَيَّ خُطُوبُهَا
إِذَا عِبْتُ مِنْهُ خَلَّةً فَتَرَكْتُهُ دَعَتْنِي إِلَيْهِ خَلَّةٌ لَا أَعِيبُهَا

١٧،٤ وقال بشّار

إِذَا كُنْتَ فِي كُلِّ ٱلْأُمُورِ مُعَاتِبًا خَلِيلَكَ لَمْ تَلْقَ ٱلَّذِي لَا تُعَاتِبُهْ
فَعِشْ وَاحِدًا أَوْ صِلْ أَخَاكَ فَإِنَّهُ مُقَارِفُ ذَنْبٍ مَرَّةً وَمُجَانِبُهْ
إِذَا أَنْتَ لَمْ تَشْرَبْ مِرَارًا عَلَى ٱلْقَذَى ظَمِئْتَ وَأَيُّ ٱلنَّاسِ تَصْفُو مَشَارِبُهْ

its basis is affectation, and its outcome is distasteful criticism. A eulogy is most useful to the author and profitable for its subject, lasting in its effect and well-remembered, if it is true and appropriate to the manifest standing of the person praised so that the sole end of the description will be to draw attention to him.

I maintain that if it is impossible to record the virtues of the Turks other than by noting the defects of the other troops, it would be more proper and prudent not to mention any of them and to abandon this treatise altogether. Describing some groups favorably hardly compensates for portraying others unflatteringly, for to speak well of the majority is expected and should go without saying, while to speak ill of the minority is a sin and a failure to do one's duty. Surely a small dose of obligatory duty is more beneficial for us than a great deal of supererogatory service. Everyone has a share of shortcomings and a measure of sinful deeds, and the only thing that makes one person better than another is having more good than bad qualities. Certainly, no one is known to possess all virtues and to be free of all defects, whether great or small, open or secret. 4.14

On this topic, al-Nābighah said: 4.15

You are not protecting a friend when you don't set right
his failings, for what man is perfect?

Al-Ḥarīsh al-Saʿdī said: 4.16

I have a comrade whose friendship is like the days of my life,
its forms coloring my existence.
Were I to censure one quality in him and then leave him,
another quality unreproved calls me back to him.

Bashshār said: 4.17

Were you to rebuke your friend for everything,
would you find anyone not to fault?
So either live alone or be at peace with your friend, for
he may yield to sin once but shun it later.
If you won't ever drink water with a little dirt in it,
you will go thirsty, for whose drink is always pure?

وقال مطيع بن إياس الليثيّ ١٨،٤

وَلَئِنْ كُنْتَ لَا تُصَاحِبُ إِلَّا صَاحِبًا لَا تَزِلُّ مَا عَاشَ نَعْلُهْ
لَمْ تَجِدْهُ وَلَوْ جَهَدْتَ وَأَيْنَ بِٱلَّذِي لَا يَكُونُ يُوجَدُ مِثْلُهْ
إِنَّمَا صَاحِبِي ٱلَّذِي يَغْفِرُ ٱلذَّنْ بَ وَيَكْفِيهِ مِنْ أَخِيهِ أَقَلُّهْ

وقال محمّد بن سعيد وهو رجل من الجند ١٩،٤

سَأَشْكُرُ عَمْرًا إِنْ تَرَاخَتْ مَنِيَّتِي أَيَادِيَ لَمْ تُمْنَنْ وَإِنْ هِيَ جَلَّتِ
فَتًى غَيْرُ مَحْجُوبِ ٱلْغِنَى عَنْ صَدِيقِهِ وَلَا مُظْهِرُ ٱلشَّكْوَى إِذَا ٱلنَّعْلُ زَلَّتِ
رَأَى خَلَّتِي مِنْ حَيْثُ يَخْفَى مَكَانُهَا فَكَانَتْ قَذَى عَيْنَيْهِ حَتَّى تَجَلَّتِ

فإذا كان الخلطاء من جمهور الناس وأهل المقاييس[١] من دهماء الجماعة يرون ذلك واجبًا في الأخلاق ومصلحة في المعاش وتدبيرًا في التعامل على ما فيهم من مشاركة الخطأ للصواب وامتزاج الضعف بالقوّة فلسنا نشكّ أنّ الإمام الأكبر والرئيس الأعظم مع الأعراق الكريمة والأخلاق الرفيعة والتمام في الحلم والعلم والكمال في الحزم والعزم مع التمكين والقدرة والفضيلة والرياسة والسيادة والخصائص التي معه من التوفيق والعصمة والتأييد وحسن المعونة لم يكن الله ليجلّله لباس الخلافة ويحبوه ببهاء الإمامة وبأعظم نعمة وأسبغها وأفضل كرامة وأسناها ثمّ وصل طاعته بطاعته ومعصيته بمعصيته إلّا ومعه من الحلم في موضع الحلم والعفو في موضع العفو والتغافل في موضع التغافل ما لا يبلغه فضل ذي فضل ولا حلم ذي حلم ٢٠،٤

١ أهل المقاييس: د: أصحاب المعايش.

Muṭīʿ ibn Iyās al-Laythī said: 4.18

If you wish only to be friends
with someone who never puts a foot wrong,
you will find no one, however hard you strive.
What can one do about someone whose type doesn't exist?
Rather, my friend is someone who forgives a fault,
content that his companion seldom errs.

Muḥammad ibn Saʿīd, a soldier, said: 4.19

I will thank ʿAmr, if my fate allows me time,
for favors granted ungrudgingly, though considerable.
A man whose wealth is not held back from his friend,
and who makes no show of complaint when his friend's sandal slips.
He saw my failing when it was still hidden
but bore with it until it was remedied.

The bulk of society and the majority of people consider human fallibility to be a moral necessity, a positive benefit in everyday life, and sound policy in their dealings with one another, despite the general tendency to conflate wrong with right and to mix weakness and strength. We can, therefore, have no doubt that in the case of the great imam, the mighty leader with his noble ancestral origins, his exalted moral nature, wholly clement and wise, perfect in prudence and resolve, endowed with authority, power, excellence, and leadership, and with his special characteristics of divine fortune, protection, support, and sustenance, God would never have conferred upon him the dignity and splendor of the caliphal office and the most exalted degree of grace and honor, and then made obedience or disobedience to him equivalent to obedience or disobedience to Himself, if He had not also empowered him to forgive, pardon, and overlook failings, wherever justified, to a degree beyond anyone else's virtue and clemency. 4.20

١،٥ ونحن قائلون ولا حول ولا قوّة إلّا بالله العظيم فيما انتهى إلينا من القول في الأتراك زعم محمّد بن الجهم وثمامة بن أشرس والقاسم بن سيّار في جماعة ممّن يغشى دار الخلافة وهي دار العامّة قالوا جميعًا بينا حميد بن عبد الحميد جالسًا ومعه إخشيد الصغديّ وأبو شجاع شبيب بن بخارا خداي البلخيّ ويحيى بن معاذ ورجال من المعدودين المتقدّمين في العلم بالحرب من أصحاب التجارب والمراس وطول المعالجة والمعاناة بصناعة الحرب إذ خرج رسول المأمون فقال لهم يقول لكم مفترقين ومجتمعين ليثبت كلّ رجل منكم دعواه وحجّته ويقول لكم أيّما أحبّ إلى كلّ قائد منكم إذا كان في مائة من نخبته وثقاته أن يلقى بهم مائة تركيّ أو مائة خارجيّ فقال القوم جميعًا نلقي مائة تركيّ أحبّ إلينا من أن نلقى مائة خارجيّ

٢،٥ وحميد ساكت فلمّا فرغ القوم جميعًا من حججهم قال الرسول لحميد قد قال القوم فقل واكتب قولك وليكن حجّة لك أو عليك قال بل ألقى مائة خارجيّ أحبّ إليّ لأنّني وجدت الخصال التي يفضل بها الخارجيّ والتركيّ جميع المقاتلة غير تامّة في الخارجيّ ووجدتها تامّة في التركيّ ففضل التركيّ على الخارجيّ بقدر فضل الخارجيّ على سائر المقاتلة ثمّ بان التركيّ من الخارجيّ بأمور ليس فيها للخارجيّ دعوى ولا متعلّق على أنّ هذه الأمور التي بان بها التركيّ من الخارجيّ أعظم خطرًا وأكثر نفعًا ممّا شاركه الخارجيّ في بعضه

٣،٥ ثمّ قال حميد والخصال التي يصول بها الخارجيّ على سائر الناس صدق الشدّة عند أوّل وهلة وهي الدفعة التي يبلغون بها ما أرادوا وينالون الذي أملوا والثانية الصبر على الخبب وعلى طول السرى حتّى يصبّحوا القوم غارّين فيهجموا عليهم وهم نثر ولحم على وضم فيعجّلونهم عن الرؤية وعن ردّ النفس بعد الجولة والنزوة لا

The Argument for the Superiority of Turks over Kharijites

We will now speak, God willing, of what we have heard said about the Turks. 5.1
Muḥammad ibn al-Jahm, Thumāmah ibn Ashras, and al-Qāsim ibn Sayyār, among others who frequented the palace of the Caliph al-Maʾmūn—more specifically, the public reception hall—all tell the following story. Ḥumayd ibn ʿAbd al-Ḥamīd was sitting there, in the company of Ikhshīd al-Ṣughdī, Abū Shujāʿ Shabīb ibn Bukhārākhudā al-Balkhī, Yaḥyā ibn Muʿādh, and others reckoned as prominent authorities on military matters—men of experience and professional skill, long versed in the craft of war. Suddenly a messenger from al-Maʾmūn came forward and said to them, "Al-Maʾmūn asks you, severally and collectively, to set out, each man of you, his claims and arguments in response to this question: Would any officer among you prefer, if he were with a hundred of his chosen and trusted men, to meet a hundred Turks or a hundred Kharijites?" They all replied, "We would prefer to face a hundred Turks rather than a hundred Kharijites."

Ḥumayd kept silent, and when the others had finished giving their justifica- 5.2
tions, the messenger said to Ḥumayd, "The others have spoken, so now speak and write down what you say, and let it be evidence for you or against you." So Ḥumayd said, "I would rather meet a hundred Kharijites, for I have found that the qualities by which the Kharijite and the Turk surpass all other fighters are present in the Kharijite to an imperfect degree, but they are present in the Turk to perfection. The Turk surpasses the Kharijite as much as the Kharijite surpasses other fighters. Furthermore, the Turk is distinguished from the Kharijite by the possession of some qualities that the latter cannot claim and that do not pertain to him. These qualities, which distinguish the Turk from the Kharijite, are more significant and advantageous than those the Kharijite partially shares with the Turk.

"The qualities whereby the Kharijite can overcome other men are, first, 5.3
the precision of their initial onslaught, this being the impetus by which they reach their objective and attain what they hope for. Second, there is their endurance of a long night march on horseback, so that they might sneak up on their enemy at daybreak and attack them while they are scattered and are easy prey.[45] They descend upon their victims too fast for the latter to see them[46] or get their breath back after the initial charge, never imagining that anyone could cover such a distance in so short a span of time. The third is that the

يظنّون أنّ أحدًا يقطع في ذلك المقدار من الزمان ذلك المقدار من البلاد والثالثة أنّ الخارجيّ موصوف عند الناس بأنّه إن طلب أدرك وإن طُلب فات

٤،٥ والرابعة خفّة الأزواد وقلّة الأمتعة وأنّها تجنب الخيل وتركب البغال وإن احتاجت أمست بأرض وأصبحت بأخرى وأنّهم قوم حين خرجوا لم يخلفوا الأموال الكثيرة والجنان الملتفّة والدور المشيّدة ولا ضياعًا ولا مستغلّات ولا جواري مطهّمات وأنّهم لا سلب لهم ولا مال معهم فيرغب الجند في لقائهم وإنّما هم كالطير لا تدّخر ولا تهتمّ لغد ولها في كلّ أرض من المياه والبزور ما يقوتها وإن لم تجد ذلك في بعض البلاد فأجنحتها تقرّب لها البعيد وتسهّل لها الحزون وكذلك الخوارج لا تمتنع عليهم القرى والطعم وإن تمتنع عليهم ففي بنات أعوج وبنات شحّاج وخفّة الأثقال والقوّة على طول الخبب ما يأتيها بأرزاقها وأكثر من أرزاقها

٥،٥ والخامسة أنّ الملوك إذا أرسلوا إليهم أعدادهم ليكونوا في خفّة أزوادهم وأثقالهم وليقووا على التنقّل كقوّتهم لم يقووا عليهم لأنّ مائة من الجند لا يقومون لمائة من الخوارج وإن كثّفوا الجيش وضاعفوا العدد ثقلوا عن طلبهم وعن الفوت إن طلبهم عدوّهم ومتى شاء الخارجيّ أن يقرب منهم ليتطرّفهم أو ليصيب الغرّة أو ليبيّتهم فعل ذلك ثقة بأنّه يقيم[1] عند الفرصة ورؤية العورة ويمكنه الهرب عند الخوف وإن شاء كبسهم ليقطع نظامهم أو ليقتطع القطعة منهم قال حميد فهذه هي مفاخرهم وخصالهم التي بها كره القوّاد لقاءهم

٦،٥ قال القاسم بن سيّار وخصلة أخرى وهي التي رعّبت القلوب وجنّبتها[2] ونقضت العزائم وفسختها وهو ما سمع الأجناد ومقاتلة العوامّ من ضرب المثل بالخوارج كقول الشاعر

١ أو ليبيّتهم . . . يقيم: د: منهم أو ليسلبهم وليعلم ذلك فإنّه يعم. ٢ ت، ق: حببتها؛ د: خلعتها.

Kharijite is universally portrayed as able to overtake everyone he pursues but escape from anyone who tries to pursue him.

"The fourth is their practice of traveling with light provisions and little baggage, and of leading their horses by their side while riding their mules.[47] If necessary, they can be in one region at evening and in the next by the following morning. When they go out on an expedition, they do not leave behind them great wealth, luxuriant gardens, lofty mansions, crop-bearing estates, or beauteous maidens. They possess nothing worth plundering and take no possessions with them that would entice regular troops to engage them in battle. They are like the birds of the air, which do not hoard and take no thought for the morrow. Wherever they happen to be, they have sufficient water and grains to sustain them, and if in some areas this cannot be found, their wings make long distances short and rough terrain smooth. This is how it is with the Kharijites; hospitality and sustenance are nowhere denied them, or, if denied, they have in their horses and mules, in the lightness of their burdens, and in their power to ride long distances the means to bring in supplies for themselves, more indeed than would sustain them. 5.4

"The fifth quality of the Kharijites is that even if kings send against them forces equal in numbers with the same lightness of provisions and baggage as the Kharijites, so that they might be as mobile as them, such a force will not in fact be a match for them, because a hundred regular troops cannot stand up to a hundred Kharijites. If, on the other hand, the kings reinforce the army by doubling their number, their soldiers will be too cumbersome to pursue the enemy or to take evasive action if pursued. Whenever the Kharijite chooses to come to close quarters, with the objective of harassing their flanks, catching them unawares, or attacking them by night, he does so in full confidence that he can stay if there is an opportunity and he sees a weakness in their defense, but that he can escape if the situation is perilous. And if he wishes, he can launch a surprise attack with the aim of throwing their ranks into disorder or cutting off a detachment from the main army. These," concluded Ḥumayd, "are the qualities on which they pride themselves and on account of which military commanders are loath to engage them." 5.5

Al-Qāsim ibn Sayyār here remarked, "There is also another quality, one which excites fear and aversion[48] in men's hearts, and saps and destroys resolve—namely, what regular troops and common soldiery hear in various proverbial expressions about the Kharijites uttered by poets, such as: 5.6

إِذَا مَا ٱلْبَخِيـلُ وَٱلْمُحَـاذِرُ لِلْقِـرَى رَأَى ٱلضَّيْفَ مِثْلَ ٱلْأَزْرَقِ ٱلْمُجَفَّفِ

وكقول الآخر

وَقَلْبِ وَدٍّ حَالَ عَنْ عَهْـدِهِ وَٱلسَّيْفُ يَنْبُو بِيَدِ ٱلشَّارِي

وكقول الآخر

لِقَاءُ ٱلْأُسْـدِ أَهْوَنُ مِنْ لِقَـاهُ إِذَا ٱلتَّحْكِيمُ يُسْهِرُ بِٱلْأَصِيلِ[1]

هذه زيادة القاسم بن سيار

٧،٥ فأمّا حميد فإنّه قال فأمّا الشدّة فالتركيّ فيها أحمد أثرًا وأجمع أمرًا وأحكم شأنًا لأنّ التركيّ من أجل أن تصدق شدّته ويتمكّن عزمه ولا يكون مشترك العزم ومنقسم الخواطر قد عوّد برذونه ألّا ينثني وإن ثناه أن يملأ فروجه إلى أن[2] يديره مرّة أو مرّتين وإلّا فإنّه لا يدع سننه ولا يقطع ركضه وإنّما أراد التركيّ أن يؤيس نفسه من البدوات ومن أن يعتريه التكذيب بعد الاعتزام لهول اللقاء وحبّ الحياة لأنّه إذا علم أنّه قد صيّر برذونه إلى هذه الغاية حتّى لا ينثني ولا يجيبه إلى التصرّف معه إلّا بأن يصنع شيئًا بين الصفّين فيه عطبه لم يقدم على الشدّة إلّا بعد إحكام الأمر والبصر بالعورة[3] وإنّما يريد أن يشبّه نفسه بالمحرج الذي إذا رأى أشدّ القتال لم يدع جهدًا ولم يدّخر حيلة ولينفي عن قلبه خواطر الفرار ودواعي الرجوع

٨،٥ وقال الخارجيّ عند الشدّة إنّما يعتمد على الطعان والأتراك تطعن طعن الخوارج وإن شدّ منهم ألف فارس فرموا رشقًا واحدًا صرعوا ألف فارس فما بقاء جيش على هذا النوع من الشدّ والخوارج والأعراب ليست لهم رماية مذكورة على ظهور الخيل والتركيّ يرمي الوحش والطير والبرجاس والناس والمجثّمة والمثل الموضوعة والطائر

١ وكقول الآخر . . . بالأصيل: زيدت من د. ٢ إلى أن: ت، ق: الا أن؛ د: للأمر. ٣ البصر بالعورة: د: النظر إلى العودة.

When the miser, anxious to avoid offering hospitality,
regards the guest like an armor-clad Azraqī.

"And:

Many a friendly heart changes its allegiance
when the Shārī's sword is blunted.

"And:

To meet with lions is less dreadful than to meet one
who cries, 'To God the judgment,'[49] banishing sleep at eventide."

This is the end of al-Qāsim ibn Sayyār's interpolation.

Then Ḥumayd resumed, saying, "In the battle charge, the Turk is more commendably effective, more collected in his determination, and more fixed in his resolve. For the Turk, in order that his onslaught may be unflinching and his conviction unshakable, and that he may not waver in resolution or be distracted in mind, has trained his mount never to swerve, or, if he does turn him aside, to go on at full speed[50] in the new direction until[51] he turns him again. Otherwise, he never changes his course or checks his gallop. The Turk's aim is to steel himself not to make any sudden changes of purpose nor, after a determined start, to be overcome by doubt through fear of battle and love of life. For only when he is sure that he has brought his mount to the point that it will not deviate and will respond to his command even to make a sortie between the two opposing ranks of the enemy in danger of death—only then will he launch the battle charge, and only after he has examined the situation and noted the enemy's weak spots. He wishes to act like a man with his back to the wall, who, when he sees the fighting at its fiercest, spares no effort and tries every maneuver, so that he might thus dispel from his mind any idea of flight and impulse to retreat. 5.7

"The Kharijite in battle relies solely on spear fighting. The Turks can use the spear as effectively as the Kharijite, but in addition, if a thousand of their horsemen join battle, they will fire off a single volley of arrows and mow down a thousand of the enemy cavalry. No army can withstand this kind of assault. The Kharijites and Bedouin Arabs have no skill worth mentioning in shooting on horseback, but the Turk can shoot at wild animals, birds, rings on a spear, people, sitting targets, dummy figures, and even birds in flight. 5.8

الخاطف ويرمي وقد ملأ فروج دابّته مدبرًا ومقبلاً ويمنة ويسرة وصعدًا وسفلاً ويرمي بعشرة أسهم قبل أن يفوّق الخارجيّ سهمًا واحدًا ويركض دابّته منحدرًا من جبل أو متسفّلاً إلى بطن واد بأكثر ممّا يمكن الخارجيّ على بسيط الأرض والتركيّ له أربعة أعين عينان في وجهه وعينان في قفاه

٩،٥ وللخارجيّ عيب في مستدبر الحرب وللخراسانيّ عيب في مستقبل الحرب فعيب الخراسانيّة أنّ لها جولة عند أوّل الالتقاء فإن ركبوا أكساءهم كانت هزيمتهم وكثيرًا ما يثوبون وذاك بعد الخطار بالعسكر وإطماع العدوّ في الشدّة والخوارج إذا ولّوا فقد ولّوا وليس لهم بعد الفرّ كرّ إلّا ما لا يعدّ والتركيّ ليست له جولة الخراسانيّ وإذا أدبر فهو السمّ الناقع والحتف القاضي لأنّه يصيب بسهمه وهو مدبر كما يصيب بسهمه وهو مقبل

١٠،٥ ولا يؤمن وهقه ولا انتساف الفرس واختطاف الفارس بتلك الركضة ولم يفلت من الوهق في جميع الدهر إلّا المهلّب بن أبي صفرة والحريش بن هلال وعبّاد بن الحصين وربّما رمى بالوهق وله فيه تدبير آخر وإن لم يجب المرميّ معه يوهم الجاهل أنّ ذلك إنّما كان لخرق التركيّ أو لحذق المرميّ[1] قال وهم علّموا الفرسان حمل قوسين وثلاثة قسيّ ومن الأوتار على حسب ذلك قال والتركيّ في حال شدّته معه كلّ شيء يحتاج إليه لنفسه وسلاحه ودابّته وأداة دابّته فأمّا الصبر على الخبب ومواصلة السير وعلى طول السرى وقطع البلاد فعجيب جدًّا[2]

١١،٥ فواحدة أنّ فرس الخارجيّ لا يصبر صبر برذون التركيّ والخارجيّ لا يحسن أن يعالج فرسه إلّا معالجة الفرسان لخيولهم والتركيّ أحذق من البيطار وأجود تقويمًا لبرذونه على ما يريده من الراضة وهو استنتجه وهو ربّاه فلوًا ويتبعه إن سمّاه وإن ركض ركض خلفه قد عوّده حتّى عرفه كما يعرف الفرس أجذم والناقة حلّي والجمل جاه والبغل عدس والحمار سأسأ وكما يعرف المجنون لقبه والصبيّ اسمه ولو حصّلت

١ ولا انتساف . . . المرميّ: زيدت من د. ٢ فعجيب جدًّا: زيدت من د.

While at a gallop, he can shoot forward or backward, left or right, upward or downward, and discharge ten arrows before the Kharijite can send up even one. He races his horse down a mountainside, or headlong into a deep ravine, faster than the Kharijite can ride on level ground. The Turk has four eyes, two in front and two in the back of his neck.

“The Kharijite has a fault in the latter phases of a battle; the Khurasani has a fault in the early phase. The fault of the Khurasanis is that they can launch a charge when battle is first joined but are routed if they then have to fall back. They may indeed rally, but only after imperiling the whole army and emboldening the enemy to make a fresh assault. The Kharijites, if they once turn tail, have done so for good, and only on very rare occasions do they regroup after flight. The Turk does not employ the same tactics as the Khurasani: When he turns in flight, it is then that he is at his most lethal and deadly, for he can shoot his arrow when facing backward just as well as he can when going forward. 5.9

“Moreover, no one is safe from his lasso, or from a horse being brought down by it, unseating the rider while at a gallop. Only al-Muhallab ibn Abī Ṣufrah, al-Ḥarīsh ibn Hilāl, and ʿAbbād ibn al-Ḥuṣayn have ever escaped their lasso. Sometimes the Turk throws the lasso having some other plan in mind, and then, just because he does not bring the lassoed victim with him, an ignorant observer might imagine that this was due to his incompetence and the victim’s cleverness. They have taught their cavalrymen to carry two or three bows with a corresponding supply of bowstrings. The Turk brings with him into battle everything he needs: his weapons, his horse, and his horse’s equipment. He is a marvel at enduring marches on horseback with no break, long night journeys, and overland treks. 5.10

“Another point is that the Kharijite horse has not the same endurance as even a workhorse of the Turks, and the Kharijite is only as good as the average cavalryman at handling horses. The Turk has more skill than a professional vet and he is better than any professional horsebreaker at training his mount in the way he wishes, since he has himself bred and raised it as a colt, so that it responds to him when he calls it and trots after him as he rides. He has trained it to do this until it knows it in the same way as any horse knows the command *ajdhim*, the she camel *ḥallī*, the male camel *jāh*, the mule *ʿadas*, and the ass *saʾsaʾ*, and in the same way as the fool knows his 5.11

مدّة عمر التركيّ وحسبت أيّامه لوجدت جلوسه على ظهر دابّته أكثر من جلوسه على ظهر الأرض

١٢،٥ والتركيّ يركب فحلًا أو رمكة ويخرج غازيًا أو مسافرًا أو متباعدًا في طلب صيد أو سبب من الأسباب فتتبعه الرمكة وأفلاؤها إن أعياه اصطياد الناس اصطاد الوحش وإن أخفق منها واحتاج إلى طعام فصدّ دابّة من دوابّه وإن عطش حلب رمكة من رماكه وإن أراح واحدة ركب أخرى من غير أن ينزل إلى الأرض وليس في الأرض أحد إلّا وبدنه ينتقض من اقتيات اللحم وحده غيره وكذلك دابّته تكتفي بالعنقر والعشب والشجر لا يظلّها من شمس ولا يكنّها من برد

١٣،٥ قال وأمّا الصبر على الخبب فإنّ الثغريّين والفرانقيّين والخصيان والخوارج لو اجتمعت قواهم في شخص واحد لما وفوا بتركيّ واحد والتركيّ لا يبقى معه على طول الغاية إلّا الصميم من دوابّه والذي يقتله التركيّ بإتعابه له ويبقيه عند غزاته هو الذي لا يصبر معه فرس الخارجيّ ولا يبقى معه كلّ برذون بخاريّ ولو ساير خارجيًّا لاستفرغ جهده قبل أن يبلغ الخارجيّ عفوه

١٤،٥ والتركيّ هو الراعي وهو السائس وهو الرائض وهو النخّاس وهو البيطار وهو الفارس والتركيّ الواحد أمّة على حدة قال وإذا سار التركيّ في غير عساكر الترك فسار القوم عشرة أميال سار عشرين ميلًا لأنّه ينقطع عن العسكر يمنة ويسرة في ذرى الجبال ويستبطن قعور الأودية في طلب الصيد وهو في ذلك يرمي كلّ ما دبّ ودرج وطار ووقع قال والتركيّ لم يسر في العساكر سير الناس قطّ ولا سار مستقيمًا قطّ

١٥،٥ قال وإذا طالت الدلجة واشتدّ السير وبعد المنزل وانتصف النهار واشتدّ التعب وشغل الناس الكلال وصمت المتسايرون فلم ينطقوا وقطعهم ما هم فيه من التشاغل بالحديث وتفسّخ كلّ شيء من شدّة الحرّ وجمد كلّ شيء من شدّة[١] البرد وتمنّى كلّ جليد القويّ على طول السرى أن تُطوى له الأرض وكلّما رأى خيالًا أو علمًا

١ الحرّ . . . من شدّة: زيدت من د.

nickname or the child its name.[52] If you were to calculate the Turk's lifespan and reckon up his days, you would find that he had spent more time in the saddle than on firm ground.

“The Turk rides a stallion or a mare, and when he goes out on a raid or a journey or an extended hunting trip, or whatever it may be, the mare and her foals follow him. If he is unable to hunt men for booty, he hunts wild animals; if he is unsuccessful in that and needs food, he bleeds one of his beasts, and if he is thirsty, he milks one of his mares. When he wants to rest one of them, he mounts another without setting foot to ground. There is nobody on earth whose health is not impaired by a meat-only diet except for the Turk. Similarly, his horse can make do with roots, grasses, and shrubs, and survive without shade from the sun or shelter from the cold. 5.12

“When it comes to the endurance of a long trek, even if the strength of the frontier guards, the postal couriers, the eunuchs, and the Kharijites were to be united in one person, they would be no match for a single Turk. Only the purebred among the Turk's horses can last to the end of a long journey with him. Even the beast the Turk rides to death, or the one he spares as unfit from his raiding expeditions, is one the Kharijite horse could not hold its own against, nor any Bukharan steed keep up with. If the Turk were to accompany a Kharijite on a journey, he would have exerted himself to the utmost before the Kharijite had even gotten going. 5.13

“The Turk is the breeder, groom, trainer, smith,[53] vet, and rider—a whole community all by himself. If the Turk marches in an army of non-Turks, he goes twenty miles where the others go ten, because he breaks off from the main army to ride away on the right or left flank, scaling the peaks of mountains and descending deep into the valleys in quest of game, in pursuit of which he will shoot anything that crawls, walks, flies, or lands. Thus, the Turk does not move with the army as other men do, for he never proceeds in a straight line. 5.14

“Imagine an occasion when a start is made before dawn on a punishing march, with the camp far distant, and midday comes, bringing with it desperate exhaustion. Everyone is so overcome with weariness that silence reigns among the marchers and they do not utter a word because they are too preoccupied with their own plight to engage in conversation. Everything around is cracked with intense heat or frozen solid with intense cold, and every sturdy 5.15

استبشر به[1] وظنّ أنّه قد بلغ المنزل فإذا بلغه الفارس نزل وهو متفحّج كأنّه صبيّ مختون يئنّ أنين المريض ويستريح إلى التثاؤب ويتداوى ممّا به بالتمطّي والتضجّع وترى التركيّ في تلك الحال وقد سار ضعف ما ساروا وقد أتعب منكبيه كثرة النزع يرى بقرب المنزل عيرًا أو ظبيًا أو عرض له ثعلب أو أرنب كيف يركض ركض مبتدىء مستأنف كأنّ الذي سار ذلك السير وتعب ذلك التعب غيره

١٦،٥ وإن بلغ الناس واديًا فازدحموا على مسلكه أو على قنطرته بطن برذونه فأقحمه ثمّ طلع من الجانب الآخر كأنّه كوكب وإن انتهوا إلى عقبة صعبة ترك السنن وذهب في الجبل صعدًا ثمّ تدلّى من موضع يعجز عنه الوعل وأنت تحسبه مخاطرًا بنفسه للذي ترى من مطلعه ولو كان في كلّ ذلك مخاطرًا ما دامت له السلامة مع تتابع ذلك منه

١٧،٥ قال ويفخر الخارجيّ بأنّه إذا طلب أدرك وإذا طُلب فات والتركيّ ليس يحوج إلى أن يفوت لأنّه لا يُطلب ولا يُرام ومن يروم ما لا يُطمع فيه

١٨،٥ فهذا دليل على أنّا قد علمنا أنّ العلّة التي عمّت الخوارج بالنجدة استواء حالاتهم في الديانة وأشدّ اعتقادهم بأنّ القتال دين لأنّنا حين وجدنا السجستانيّ والجزريّ واليماميّ والمغربيّ والعمانيّ والأزرقيّ منهم والنجديّ والإباضيّ والصفريّ والمولى والعربيّ والعجميّ والأعرابيّ والعبيد والنساء والحائك والفلّاح كلّهم يقاتل مع اختلاف الأنساب وتباين البلدان علمنا أنّ الديانة هي التي سوّت بينهم في ذلك كما أنّ كلّ حجّام في الأرض من أيّ جنس كان ومن أهل أيّ بلد كان فهو يحبّ النبيذ وكما أنّ أصحاب الخلقان والسمّاكين والنخّاسين والحاكة في كلّ بلد ومن كلّ جنس شرار خلق الله في المبايعة والمعاملة فعلمنا بذلك أنّ ذلك خلقة في هذه الصناعات وبنية في هذه التجارات حتّى صاروا من بين جميع الناس كذلك

١ أو علمًا استبشر به: د: أو أبصر علمًا سرّ به واستبشر.

man, though strong in the long night march, yearns for the ground to swallow him up. Every time he sees a boundary stone or a route marker, he hails it with joy, thinking he has reached camp. And when he does reach camp, the horseman dismounts, his legs bowed[54] like a young eunuch, and he groans like a sick man, relaxes in a yawn, and recovers by lying down at full stretch. In such a situation, you will notice that the Turk, who has traveled twice as far as the rest, and wearied his shoulders by frequently drawing his bow, upon spotting close to the camp a wild ass or gazelle or a fox or hare, gallops off as if he is starting his journey afresh so that it hardly seems he is the person who made that exhausting journey.

“When the people reach a wadi and bunch together at the path through it, or the bridge, the Turk digs his spurs into his horse's belly and rides him straight at it and then comes up on the other side like a rising star. If they come to a steep path in the mountains, he leaves the track and goes straight up the mountainside and then hurtles down from some spot inaccessible even to the ibex. From what you can see of his ascent, you would think he was risking his life, and yet if he really was putting himself in danger by all this, he would not last long given how often he does it. 5.16

“The Kharijite boasts that when he pursues, he overtakes, and if pursued, he escapes. However, the Turk has no need to get away, because nobody ever seeks to pursue him, for who tries to attain the unattainable? 5.17

“Furthermore, it is a fact well known that what universally inspires the Kharijites with valor is their unanimity in faith and their strong conviction that fighting is a religious act. For when we find that the Sijistānī, Jazarī, Yamāmī,[55] Maghribī, Omani, Azraqī, Najdī, Ibāḍī, Ṣufrī, Mawla, Arab, Persian, Bedouin, slaves, women, weaver, and farmer all fight despite the differences in their social groupings and geographical origins, we recognize that it is religion which forms the integrating factor among them. Similarly, every cupper[56] on earth, whatever his race or country, loves wine; so too, rag merchants, fishermen, slave traders, and weavers in any country and of every race are the most despicable of God's creation when it comes to trading and dealing. From this, we may conclude that such a character and disposition are intrinsic to those professions and trades, so that they are like this everywhere in the world. 5.18

١٩،٥ قال ورأيناه في بلاده ليس يقاتل على دين ولا على تأويل ولا على ملك ولا على خراج ولا على عصبيّة ولا على غيرة دون الحرمة ولا على حميّة ولا على عداوة ولا على وطن ومنع دار ولا مال وإنّما يقاتل على السلب والخيار في يده وليس يخاف الوعيد إن هرب ولا يرجو الوعد إن أبلى عذرًا وكذلك هم في بلادهم وغاراتهم وحروبهم وهو الطالب غير المطلوب ومن كان كذلك فإنّما يأخذ العفو من قوّته ولا يحتاج إلى مجهوده ثمّ مع ذلك لا يقوم له شيء ولا يطمع فيه أحد فما ظنّك بمن هذه صفته لو[1] اضطرّه إحراج أو غيرة أو غضب أو تديّن أو عرض له بعض ما يصحب المقاتل المحامي من العلل والأسباب

٢٠،٥ قال وقناة الخارجيّ طويلة صمّاء وقناة التركيّ مطرّد أجوف والقُنيّ الجوف القصار أشدّ طعنة وأخفّ محملاً والعجم تجعل القنيّ الطوال للرجّالة وهي قنيّ الأبناء على أبواب الخنادق والمضايق والأبناء في هذا الباب لا يجرون مع الأتراك والخراسانيّة لأنّ الغالب على الأبناء المطاعنة على أبواب الخنادق وفي المضايق وهؤلاء أصحاب الخيل والفرسان وعلى أصحاب الخيل والفرسان يدور أمر الجيوش لهم الكرّ والفرّ

٢١،٥ والفارس هو الذي يطوي الجيش طيّ السجلّ ويفرّقهم فرق الشعر وليس يكون الكمين ولا الطليعة ولا الساقة إلّا الكبار[2] منهم وهم أصحاب الأيّام المذكورة والحروب الكبار والفتوح العظام ولا تكون المقانب والكتائب إلّا منهم ومنهم من يحمل البنود والرايات والطبول والتجافيف والأجراس وهم أصحاب الصهيل والقتام وزجر الخيل وقعقعة الريح في الثياب والسلاح ووقع الحوافر والإدراك إذا طلبوا والفوت إذا طُلبوا ولم يجعل النبيّ صلّى الله عليه وسلّم للفارس سهمين وللراجل من المقاتلة سهمًا واحدًا إلّا لتضاعيف الردّ في القتل والفتوح والنهبة والمغانم

١ ت: أو لو؛ د: أن لو. ٢ زيدت من ق.

"However, we have observed that the Turk in his own country never fights for religion or sect, kingship or taxes, or for partisan reasons or jealousy, unless it concerns women, or out of anger or enmity, or for the homeland, or in defense of home and property. Rather, he fights solely for plunder insofar as the choice is his. He does not fear any threat if he should flee nor hope for any reward if he achieves victory.[57] This is how they are in their own country, in their own raids and wars. The Turk is always the pursuer, never the pursued. Now, a person of this type merely draws on his surplus strength and has no need to exert himself. Moreover, nothing can stand up to the Turk and nobody aspires to overcome him. So, what might one expect of someone like this if he were pressured by straitened circumstances, concern for loved ones, anger, or religious duty, or if he were subject to any of the other factors and reasons that motivate those who fight to defend a cause? 5.19

"The Kharijite lance is long and solid, while the Turk's is hollow and like a short stabbing spear, for short, hollow lances make for a more effective thrust as well as being lighter to carry. The Persians assign long lances to the infantry, and such lances are also used by the Banawis at the entrances of trenches and in confined spaces. In this respect, however, the Banawis do not compare with the Turks and Khurasanis, for the Banawis mostly engage in close-quarter thrusting at the access points to ditches and narrow passes, whereas the former two are cavalrymen, and it is on cavalrymen that the fate of armies depends when they engage in charge and retreat. 5.20

"The cavalry can turn back an enemy army like rolling up a scroll or drive a wedge through it like parting hair. For that reason, the best cavalrymen make up an ambush or an advance party or a rearguard, those who are veterans of celebrated battles, great wars, and glorious conquests. It is from them that special mounted troops and squadrons are formed, and it is they who carry the banners, flags, and drums, and wear chain mail and bells. They are at home with the neighing of their steeds, the dust clouds of the battlefield, the shouts of encouragement to the horses, the sound of the wind whistling through their garments, the clash of arms, and the thunder of hooves. They overtake when in pursuit and escape when pursued. The reason the Prophet assigned two shares of the booty to each cavalryman and just one to the infantryman was simply because of the former's doubled effectiveness in killing, conquest, spoil, and booty. 5.21

٢٢٫٥ ثمّ قال ولعمري إنّ للأبناء من القتال في السكك والسجون والمضايق ما ليس لغيرهم ولكنّ الرجّالة أبدًا أتباع ومأمورون ومنقادون وقائد الرجّالة لا يكون فارسًا وقائد الفرسان من الممتنع أن يكون راجلًا ومن تعوّد الطعان والضرب والرمي راكبًا إن اضطرّ إلى الطعن والضرب والرمي راجلًا كان على ذاك أدفع عن نفسه وأردّ عن أصحابه من الراجل إذا احتاج أن يستعمل سلاحه فارسًا وعلى أنّه ما أكثر ما ينزلون ويقاتلون وقد قال الشاعر

لَمْ تُطِيقُوا أَنْ تَنْزِلُوا وَنَزَلْنَا   وَأَخُو ٱلْحَرْبِ مَنْ أَطَاقَ ٱلنُّزُولَا

وقال الضبّيّ

وَعَلَامَ أَرْكَبُهُ إِذَا لَمْ أَنْزِلِ

وقال آخر

فَمُعَانِقٌ وَمُنَازِلُ

٢٣٫٥ وقال حميد وليس في الأرض قوم إلّا والتساند في الحروب والاشتراك في الرياسة ضارّ لهم إلّا الأتراك على أنّ الأتراك لا يتساندون ولا يتشاركون وذلك أنّ الذي يُكره من المساندة والمشاركة اختلاف الرأي والتنافس في السرّ والتحاسد بين الأشكال والتواكل فيما بين المشتركين والأتراك إذا صافّوا جيشًا وإن كان في القوم موضع عورة فكلّهم قد أبصرها وعرفها وإن لم تكن هناك عورة ولم يكن فيهم مطمع وكان الرأي الانصراف فكلّهم قد رأى ذلك الرأي وعرف الصواب فيه وخواطرهم واحدة ودواعيهم مستوية بإقبالهم معًا وليس هم أصحاب تأويلات ولا أصحاب تفاخر وتناشد وإنّما شأنهم إحكام أمرهم فالاختلاف يقلّ بينهم وكانت الفرس تعيب العرب إذا خرجوا إلى الحرب متساندين وكانت تقول الاشتراك في الحرب

"It is true, of course, that the Banawis are unrivaled at fighting in streets, enclosed spaces,[58] and narrow passes. Nevertheless, the infantry are always subordinates, acting under the command and leadership of others; the captain of the infantry is not usually a horseman, but the captain of the cavalry must absolutely not be a foot soldier. A man trained to employ the spear, sword, and bow when mounted, if compelled to do the same on foot, is better able to defend himself and his comrades than the infantryman obliged to use his weapon on horseback. Furthermore, the cavalry very commonly dismounts and fights hand to hand, as the poet says: 5.22

You could not endure dismounted combat, but we did,
and the true warrior is he who can do so.

"And al-Ḍabbī says:

Why should I ride my horse if I am not going to dismount to fight?

"And another says:

Oh, for a hand-to-hand fighter and one eager to dismount to fight!"

Ḥumayd continued, saying, "Every people on earth is impaired by combined operations and shared command except for the Turks, since they do not in fact adopt these practices. What is disagreeable about combined operations and sharing of command is that it leads to divisions of opinion, secret rivalries, mutual jealousies between equals in rank, and the offloading of responsibilities among the participants in the command. When the Turks are drawn up in their battle ranks, they all see and recognize if there is a weak spot in the opposing force. If the sensible thing is to withdraw because there is no weak spot or hope of gain, every Turk makes the same assessment and recognizes that it is the right thing to do in that situation. Their ideas and tactics are completely at one when they make a united advance. They are not given to suspicions of others or competitive boasting or rivalrous versifying; their nature is to present a solid front, and there is rarely dissension among them. The Persians have always reproached the Arabs for going to war with combined forces, saying: 'Shared decision-making in war, marriage, and government is equally bad.' So, what do you think then," said Ḥumayd, "of a people who can engage 5.23

وفي الزوجة وفي الإمرة سواء وقال حميد فما ظنّك بقوم إذا تساندوا لم يضرّهم التساند فكيف يكونون إذا تحاشدوا

٢٤،٥ فلمّا انتهى الخبر إلى المأمون قال ليست بالترك حاجة إلى حكم حاكم بعد حميد فإنّ حميدًا قد مارس الفريقين وحميد خراسانيّ وحميد عربيّ فليس للتهمة عليه طريق قالوا وأتى الخبر ذا اليمينين طاهر بن الحسين فقال ما أحسن ما قال حميد أما إنّه لم يقصّر ولم يفرّط فهذا قول الخليفة المأمون وحكم حميد وتصويب طاهر

١،٦ وخبّرني رجل من أهل خراسان أو من بني سدوس قال سمعت أبا البطّ يقول ويلكم كيف أصنع بفارس يملأ فروج دابّته منحدرًا من جبل أو مصعدًا في مقطع عفير ويمكنه على ظهر الفرس ما لا يمكن الرقّاص الأبليّ على ظهر الأرض

٢،٦ قال وقال سعيد بن عقبة بن سلم الهنائيّ وكان ذا رأي في الحرب وابن ذي رأي فيها فرق ما بيننا وبين الترك أنّ الترك لم تغز قومًا قطّ ولا صافت جيشًا ولا هجمت على عدوّ كانوا عربًا أو عجمًا فأخرجوا إليهم أعدادهم ولقوهم بمثلهم وليس غايتهم إلّا أن ينقادوا ليكفّوا عنهم بأسهم ومعرّتهم ويصرفوا عنهم كيدهم فإن هم امتنعوا من الصلح واعتزموا إلى الحرب فليس شأنهم والذي يدور عليه أمرهم إلّا منع أنفسهم وتحصين عسكرهم والاحتراس منهم فأمّا أن ترقى هممهم أو تسمو أنفسهم إلى الاحتيال عليهم والتماس غرّتهم فإنّ هذا شيء لا يخطر على بال من يحاربهم ثمّ قال وقد عرفتم حيلهم في دخول المدن من جهة حيطانها المصمتة العريضة وحيلتهم في عبور نهر بلخ

٣،٦ وسعيد هذا هو الذي قال إذا حاربتم وكنتم ثلاثة فاجعلوا واحدًا مددًا وآخر كمينًا وله كلام في الحرب غير هذا كثير قال سعيد وأخبرني أبي قال شهدت أبا الخطّاب يزيد بن قتادة بن دعامة الفقيه وذكر قول عمر بن الخطّاب رضي الله عنه في الترك حيث قال عدوّ شديد طلبه قليل سلبه

in combined operations without detriment, and how effective will they be when their forces come together?"

When al-Ma'mūn learned of Ḥumayd's speech, he said, "The Turks need no other arbitrator to give a ruling other than Ḥumayd, for Ḥumayd has experience of both parties. He is himself a Khurasani and an Arab, and so there is no way that he can be impugned." The report also reached Dhū l-Yamīnayn Ṭāhir ibn al-Ḥusayn, and he observed, "How well Ḥumayd has expressed himself; his words are neither too terse nor too excessive." Such was the comment of the Caliph al-Ma'mūn on Ḥumayd's assessment of the Turks and Ṭāhir's endorsement of it. 5.24

Reports Recounted to al-Jāḥiz About the Turks

A Khurasani or Sadūsī tribesman told me that he had heard Abū l-Baṭṭ say, "How on earth can I cope with a horseman who can gallop at full tilt down a mountainside or up a dry watercourse, and perform on horseback feats that a dancer from Ubullah cannot do on the firm ground?" 6.1

Saʿīd ibn ʿUqbah ibn Salm al-Hunāʾī, a man of good judgment on military affairs, as was his father before him, remarked, "The difference between us and the Turks is that the latter have never raided a people or taken up battle positions to launch an attack on enemy troops, be they Arab or non-Arab, by deploying a force that was equally matched in numbers. For the sole aim of the Turks is to make their opponents submit in order to spare themselves any harm, abuse, or mischief. If these opponents then reject a peace treaty and decide to fight it out, the Turks' whole strategy revolves around self-defense and the integrity and preservation of their army. As for any aspiration or hope of outwitting the Turks or catching them unawares, such a thing never enters the minds of their adversaries on the battlefield. You must acknowledge," added Saʿīd, "the dexterity of the Turks in gaining entry to towns over broad walls lacking any opening or foothold, and their expertise in crossing the Balkh River." 6.2

This same Saʿīd is the author of the saying, "If there are three of you going to war, hold one man in reserve and place a second in ambush," as well as many other adages about warfare. Saʿīd further reported that his father told him that he had personally heard Abū l-Khaṭṭāb Yazīd, son of Qatādah ibn Diʿāmah the jurist, narrate a saying of ʿUmar ibn al-Khaṭṭāb about the Turks—namely, "They are an enemy hard to catch and yielding little booty." 6.3

٤،٦ فقال رجل من العالية نهى عمر أبا زبيد الطائيّ عن وصف الأسد لأنّ ذاك ممّا يزيد في رعب الجبان وفي هول الجنان ويقلّ من رغب الشجاع وقد وُصف الترك بأشدّ من وصف أبي زبيد الأسد

٥،٦ وقال سعيد في حديثه يومئذ وقد قطعت شرذمة منهم بلاد أبي خزيمة يريد حمزة بن أدرك الخارجيّ وما والى خراسان في بعض الأمر وحمزة في معظم الناس فقال لأصحابه أفرجوا لهم ما تركوكم ولا تتعرّضوا لهم فإنّه قد قيل تاركوهم ما تاركوكم فهذا قول سعيد بن عقبة ورأيه وحديثه وهو عربيّ خراسانيّ

٦،٦ وذكر يزيد بن مزيد الوقعة التي قتل فيها يولبا التركيّ الوليد بن طريف الخارجيّ فقال في بعض ما يصف من شأن الترك ليس لبدن التركيّ على ظهر الدابّة ثقل ولا لمشيه على الأرض وقع وإنّه ليرى وهو مدبر ما لا يرى الفارس منّا وهو مقبل وهو يرى الفارس منّا صيدًا ويعدّ نفسه فهدًا ويعدّه ظبيًا ويعدّ نفسه كلبًا والله لو رُمي به في قعر بئر مكتوفًا لما أعجزته الحيلة ولولا أنّ أعمار عامّتهم تقصر دون الجبل يعني جبل حلوان ثمّ همّوا بنا لألقوا لنا شغلاً طويلاً

٧،٦ وأنشد رجل من أصحابه

هَبِ الدُّنْيا تُسَاقُ إِلَيْكَ عَفْوًا أَلَيْسَ مَصِيرُ ذَاكَ إِلَى زَوَالِ

قال أمّا التركيّ فلأن ينال الكفاف غصبًا أحبّ إليه من أن ينال الملك عفوًا ولم يتهنّ تركيّ بطعام قطّ إلّا أن يكون صيدًا أو مغنمًا ولا يعزّ على ظهر دابّته طالبًا كان أو مطلوبًا

٨،٦ وقال ثمامة بن أشرس وكان مثل محمّد بن الجهم في كثرة ذكره للترك قال ثمامة التركيّ لا يخاف إلّا مخوفًا ولا يطمع في غير مطمع ولا يكفّه عن الطلب إلّا اليأس صرفًا ولا يدع القليل حتّى يصيب أكثر منه وان قدر أن يجمعهما لم يفرّط في واحد منهما والباب الذي لا يحسنه لا يحسن منه شيئًا والباب الذي يحسنه قد

A man from the uplands told how ʿUmar forbade Abū Zubayd al-Ṭāʾī to describe the lion, because this would make the coward more terrified and the people more afraid of the night, as well as denting the courage of even a brave man. Yet the Turks are characterized by even more terrible qualities than those Abū Zubayd spoke of in the lion. 6.4

Saʿīd also recounted how a small detachment of Turks penetrated the country of Abū Khuzaymah—that is, Ḥamzah ibn Adrak the Kharijite—and the borders of Khurasan for some purpose or other. Ḥamzah was with the main army, and he said to his men, "Give them free passage as long as they do not bother you, and do not interfere with them, for as the proverb says, 'Leave them alone so long as they leave you alone.'" Such were the views and remarks of Saʿīd ibn ʿUqbah, an Arab and a Khurasani. 6.5

Yazīd ibn Mazyad mentioned the battle in which Yūlbā the Turk killed al-Walīd ibn Ṭarīf the Kharijite, and in describing some of the Turks' qualities he said, "On horseback the Turk's body weighs nothing, and on the march his foot hardly touches the ground. With his back turned, he can see more than one of our horsemen looking straight ahead. He deems our horsemen his prey and himself the cheetah, or our men gazelles and himself the hound. If he were thrown into the bottom of a well with his hands tied behind his back, he would still be able to find a way out. Most of them keep to the east[59] of the mountains—I mean the mountains of Ḥulwān; otherwise, if they had a mind to attack us, they would wreak complete havoc." 6.6

One of his associates quotes the verses: 6.7

Even if the world were handed to you as a gift,
will it not inevitably pass away?

He also said, "The Turk prefers to win a pittance by force than to obtain a kingdom as a favor. The only food the Turk enjoys is either game or plunder, and he is never beaten on horseback whether in pursuit or being pursued."

Thumāmah ibn Ashras—as important an authority as Muḥammad ibn al-Jahm because of how frequently he referred to the Turks—said, "The Turk fears only what is truly to be feared and strives only for what is attainable. He never gives up the chase until it is hopeless, and he only abandons a lesser quarry if he encounters a bigger one; and if he can possibly secure both together, he will not renounce either. In any art he does not excel in, he is no good at it at all, but where he does excel, he has complete mastery of the 6.8

أحكمه بأسره وأمرّه عنده وخفيّه كظاهره ولا يتشاغل بشيء ليس فيه شيء ولا على نفسه من شيء فلولا أن يجمّ نفسه بالنوم لما نام على أنّ نومه مشوب باليقظة ويقظته سليمة من الوسنة ولو كان في شقّهم أنبياء وفي أرضهم حكماء وكانت هذه الخواطر قد مرّت على قلوبهم وقرعت أسماعهم لأنسوك أدب البصريّين وحكمة اليونانيّين وصنعة أهل الصين

٩،٦ وقال ثمامة عرض لنا في طريق خراسان تركيّ ومعنا قائد يصول بنفسه ورجاله وبيننا وبين التركيّ واد فسأله أن يبارزه فارس من القوم فأخرج له رجلاً لم أر قطّ أكمل منه ولا أحسن تمامًا وقوامًا منه فاحتال حتّى عبر إليه الفارس فتجاولا ساعة ولا نظنّ إلّا أنّ صاحبنا يفي بأضعافه وهو في ذلك يتباعد عنّا فبينا هما في ذلك إذ ولّى عنه التركيّ كالهارب منه وفعل ذلك في موضع ظنّنا أنّ صاحبنا قد ظهر عليه وأتبعه الفارس لا نشكّ إلّا أنّه سيأتينا برأسه أو يأتينا به مجنوبًا إلى فرسه فلم نشعر إلّا وصاحبنا قد أفلت عن فرسه وغاب عنه فنزل التركيّ إليه فأخذ سلبه وقتله ثمّ عارض فرسه فجنبه إليه معه

١٠،٦ قال ثمامة ثمّ رأيت بعد ذلك التركيّ قد جيء به أسيرًا إلى دار الفضل بن سهل فقلت له كيف صنعت يومئذ وكيف طاولته ثمّ علاك ثمّ ولّيت عنه هاربًا ثمّ قتلته قال أمّا إنّي لو شئت أن أقتله حين عبر وقد كان مقتله بارزًا لي ولكنّي احتلت عليه حتّى نحّيته عن أصحابه لأجوّزه فلا يُحال بيني وبين فرسه وسلبه قال ثمامة وإذا هو يدير الفارس من سائر الناس ويريغه كيف شاء وأحبّ قال ثمامة وقد غبرت في أيديهم أسيرًا فما رأيت كإكرامهم وتحفهم وألطافهم فهذا ثمامة بن أشرس وهو عربيّ لا يُتّهم في الإخبار عنهم

subject and knows it inside and out. He does not allow himself to be distracted by anything futile or to his disadvantage. If he did not need to sleep in order to be refreshed, he would not sleep; even when he does sleep, it is with one eye open, and when awake he never feels drowsy. If they had known any prophets or sages in their lands, and such ideas had ever entered their minds or found in them an attentive audience, you would forget the wisdom of the Basrans, the philosophy of the Greeks, and the craftsmanship of the Chinese."[60]

Thumāmah continued, "On the road to Khurasan we encountered a Turk. 6.9
We were accompanied by an impetuous commander who was quick to put both himself and his men at risk. A dry river valley separated us and the Turk. The latter requested of our commander that one of our horsemen engage him in single combat, and the commander sent out a man more perfect and finer in build and stature than anyone I have ever seen. The Turk tricked our man into crossing the valley over to his side, and they skirmished for an hour. We had no doubt that our man would outmatch him. Yet all the time the Turk moved farther and farther away, and then suddenly turned tail, apparently in flight, right at a point when we supposed that our man had already gotten the better of him. Our horseman followed the Turk, and we were sure he would either bring us back the Turk's head or bring him back tied to his horse. However, before we knew it, our man had slipped off his horse, which ran off into the distance, and the Turk had dismounted, despoiled the man, and killed him. Then he rounded up his victim's horse and made off with it, tied at his side.

Thumāmah continued, "I later saw this Turk brought in as a prisoner to the 6.10
palace of al-Faḍl ibn Sahl, and I asked him, 'How did you manage it that day? How was it that you prolonged the skirmish until he got the better of you and you fled, but then in the end you killed him?' He replied, 'Of course, if I had wanted, I could have killed him when he first crossed the valley, for he was completely vulnerable and at my mercy. However, I tricked him to draw him away from his companions so that I might get him and not be hindered from taking his horse and despoiling him into the bargain.' So," said Thumāmah, "there he was, separating our man from the rest of the group and leading him away just as he wanted. I have myself spent some time as a prisoner in their hands," remarked Thumāmah, "and I have never seen greater generosity and kindness." Such is the testimony of Thumāmah, an Arab and an unimpeachable authority on the Turks.

وأنا أخبرك أنّي قد رأيت منهم شيئًا عجيبًا وأمرًا غريبًا رأيت في بعض غزوات ١،٧
المأمون سماطي خيل على جنبتي الطريق بقرب المنزل مائة فارس من الأتراك
في الجانب الأيمن ومائة من سائر الناس في الجانب الأيسر وإذا هم قد اصطفّوا
ينتظرون مجيء المأمون وقد انتصف النهار واشتدّ الحرّ فورد عليهم وجمع الأتراك
جلوس على ظهور خيولهم إلّا ثلاثة أو أربعة وجميع تلك الأخلاط من الجند قد رموا
بنفوسهم إلى الأرض إلّا ثلاثة أو أربعة فقلت لصاحب لي انظر أيّ شيء اتّفق لنا
أشهد أنّ المعتصم كان أعرف بهم حين جمعهم واصطنعهم

وأردت مرّة القاطول وهي المباركة وأنا خارج من بغداد وأرى فوارس من أهل ٢،٧
خراسان والأبناء وغيرهم من أصناف الجند قد عار لهم فرس وهم على خيل عتاق
يريغونه فلا يقدرون على أخذه ومرّ تركيّ ولم يكن من ذوي هيئاتهم وذوي القدر
منهم وهو على برذون له خسيس وهم على الخيول المطهّمة فاعترض الفرس اعتراضًا
وفتله فتلًا وحيًّا وأتاه من زجره بشيء فوقف أولئك الجند وصاروا نظّارة فقال
بعضهم ممّن كان يزري على ذلك التركيّ هذا وأبيك التكلّف والتعرّض أنّ فرسًا قد
أعجزهم وهم أسد البلاد وجاء هذا مع قصر قامته وضعف دابّته فطمع أن يأخذه
فما انقضى كلامه حتّى أقبل به ثمّ سلّمه إليهم ومضى لطلبته لم ينتظر ثناءهم ولا
دعاءهم ولا أراهم أنّه قد صنع شيئًا أو أتى إليهم معروفًا

والأتراك قوم لا يعرفون الملق ولا الخلابة ولا النفاق ولا السعاية ولا التصنّع ولا ٣،٧
النميمة ولا الرياء ولا البذخ على الأولياء ولا البغي على الخلطاء ولا يعرفون البدع ولم
تفسدهم الأهواء ولا يستحلّون الأموال على التأوّل وإنّما كان عيبهم والذي يوحش
منهم الحنين إلى الأوطان وحبّ التقلّب في البلدان والصبابة بالغارات والشغف
بالنهب وشدّة الإلف للعادة مع ما كانوا يتذاكرون من سرور الظفر وتتابعه

Al-Jāḥiẓ's Own Thoughts About the Turks

I[61] must tell you that I once witnessed a strange and wonderful incident involving the Turks. On one of al-Ma'mūn's expeditions, I saw two ranks of cavalry drawn up, one on each side of the road near the camp, a hundred Turks on the right and a hundred others of diverse origins on the left. There they were, all lined up, waiting for al-Ma'mūn to come. It was midday and terribly hot. Al-Ma'mūn arrived at the parade to find the Turkish contingent still in their saddles, save three or four, while all of the mixed contingent had thrown themselves to the ground, save three or four. At this, I said to a friend of mine, "Just look at what has happened; al-Muʿtaṣim certainly knew the Turks well when he enlisted them and attached them to himself." 7.1

I was once making my way to al-Qāṭūl, a blessed city, coming from Baghdad, when I saw some cavalry consisting of Khurasanis, Banawis, and other types of troops. One of their horses had broken free, and they, on noble steeds, were trying to round it up, but could not catch it. A Turk came by, in no way as well equipped or powerful as they were, mounted on a simple workhorse while the others were on splendid beasts. Yet he intercepted the runaway, heading it off with a swift turn, and he drove it along with a chiding cry while the troops stood still, looking on. One of them disparaged the Turk, saying, "What audacity! The horse has proved too much for the braves of the land, and this fellow with his stunted frame and miserable mount comes along and expects to catch it." But he had hardly finished speaking when the Turk arrived with the runaway horse, handed it over, and went off about his business without waiting for their praise or thanks, as if he had not achieved anything special or done them any favor. 7.2

The Turks, as a people, are strangers to flattery and blandishment, hypocrisy and backbiting, slander and pretense, tale-telling and dissimulation, haughtiness toward their friends and ill treatment of their associates. They know nothing of heresies and are not riven by sectarian rivalries, nor do they use legal sophistry to misappropriate people's wealth. Their one fault, and the trait that causes uneasiness, is their longing for their homeland, their love of wandering the earth, their passionate addiction to raiding and plunder, and their ingrained devotion to custom. Further, they talk constantly among themselves about the joy of victory and of repeatedly achieving it, about the sweetness of booty and of frequently amassing it, as well as about their adventurous roaming in the 7.3

وحلاوة المغنم وكثرته وملاعبهم في تلك الصحاري وتردّدهم في تلك المروج وأن لا يذهب بطول الفراغ فضل نجدتهم باطلاً ويصير حدّهم على طول الأيّام كليلاً ومن حذق شيئًا لم يصبر عنه ومن كره أمرًا فرّ منه

٤،٧ وإنّما خُصّوا بالحنين من بين جميع العجم لأنّ في تركيبهم وأخلاط طبائعهم من تركيب بلدهم وتربتهم ومشاكلة مياههم ومناسبة إخوانهم ما ليس مع أحد سواهم ألا ترى أنّك ترى البصريّ فلا تدري أبصريّ هو أم كوفيّ وترى المكّيّ فلا تدري أمكّيّ هو أم مدنيّ وترى الجبليّ فلا تدري أجبليّ هو أم خراسانيّ وترى الجزريّ فلا تدري أجزريّ هو أم شاميّ وأنت لا تغلط في التركيّ ولا تحتاج فيه إلى قيافة ولا إلى فراسة ولا إلى مساءلة ونساؤهم كرجالهم ودوابّهم تركيّة مثلهم

٥،٧ وهكذا طبع الله تلك البلدة وقسم لتلك التربة وجمع دور الدنيا ونَشْؤها إلى منتهى قواها ومدّة أجلها جارية على عللها وعلى مقدار أسبابها على قدر ما خصّها الله تعالى به وأبانها وجعل فيها فإذا صاروا إلى دار الجزاء فهي كما قال الله تعالى ﴿إِنَّا أَنشَأْنَاهُنَّ إِنشَاءً﴾ وكذلك ترى أبناء العرب والأعراب الذين نزلوا خراسان لا تفصل بين من نزل أبوه بفرغانة وبين أهل فرغانة ولا ترى بينهم فرقًا في السبال الصهب والجلود القشرة والأقفاء العظيمة والأكسية الفرغانيّة وكذلك جميع تلك الارباع لا تفصل بين أبناء النازلة وبين أبناء النابتة

٦،٧ ومحبّة الوطن شيء شامل بجميع الناس وغالب على جميع الجيرة ولكنّ ذاك في الترك أغلب وفيها أرسخ لما معها من خاصّة المشاكلة والمناسبة واستواء السنّة وتكافؤ التركيب ألا ترى أنّ العبديّ يقول عمر الله البلدان بحبّ الأوطان وأنّ ابن الزبير قال ليس الناس بشيء من أقسامهم أقنع منهم بأوطانهم وأنّ عمر ابن الخطّاب رضي الله عنه قال لولا تفرّق أهواء العباد لما عمر الله البلاد وأنّ جمعة الإياديّة قالت لولا ما أوصى الله به العباد من قفر البلاد لما وسعهم واد ولا كفاهم زاد

deserts and steppes of their homeland. Fortunately, extended leisure does not diminish their superior courage, and their keenness is not blunted by the passage of time, for anyone skilled in a thing cannot bear to be away from it, while those who hate a thing shun it.

Of all the non-Arabs, the Turks are peculiarly characterized by their longing 7.4
for their homeland, because in their constitution and temperament there are, to an extent unparalleled among other groups, affinities with the characteristics of their land and their native soil and waters, as well as with their brethren. Have you not noticed that you may see a Basran and not know whether he is Basran or Kufan, a Meccan without knowing whether he is Meccan or Medinan, a Jabalī without knowing whether he is Jabalī or Khurasani, a Jazarī without knowing whether he is Jazarī or Syrian; but you cannot make any mistake about a Turk, and do not need to apply any form of scrutiny or interrogation in his case. Their women are just like the men in this respect, as are their horses.

Such is the stamp God has placed on that country and allotted to that soil. 7.5
God brought together the families of the world, and they have expanded[62] as far as their powers and allotted lifespan allows, commensurate with the motives, occasions, and qualities selected, displayed, and implanted in them by God Almighty. When they get to the place of eternal reward, it will be as God Almighty says, «We have brought them forth as a single creation.»[63] Thus, when it comes to the descendants of the Arabs and Arab tribes who have settled in Khurasan, you will observe that you cannot distinguish between someone whose father settled in Farghānah and the natives of Farghānah; you will see they have the same blond mustaches, ruddy skins, thick necks, and Farghānī attire. The same applies in all lands: You cannot distinguish between descendants of newcomers and descendants of indigenous inhabitants.

Now, love of one's country is common to all people and prevails everywhere, 7.6
but among the Turks it is more prevalent and more deeply rooted, because of the particular closeness of their mutual affinities and relations, the uniformity of their way of life, and the homogeneity of their natures. Have you not heard al-ʿAbdī say, "God makes countries prosper through love of the homeland," while Ibn al-Zubayr said, "Nothing in our lot gives us greater contentment than our homeland." Likewise, ʿUmar ibn al-Khaṭṭāb remarked, "Were it not for the differences in our predilections, God would never have populated the world," and Jumʿat al-Īyādiyyah declared, "Had God not bidden us to traverse the earth, no valley would encompass us, no food suffice us."

وذكر قتيبة بن مسلم الترك فقال هم والله أحنّ من الإبل المعقّلة إلى أوطانها ٧،٧
لأنّ البعير يحنّ إلى وطنه وعطنه وهو بعمان من ظهر البصرة فهو يخبّ كلّ شيء ويستبطن كلّ واد حتّى يأتي مكانه على أنّه طريق لم يسلكه إلّا مرّة واحدة فلا يزال بالشمّ والاسترواح وحسن الاستدلال وبالطبيعة المخصوص بها حتّى يأتي مبركه على بعد ما بين عمان والبصرة فلذلك ضرب به قتيبة المثل والشحّ على الوطن والحنين إليه والصبابة به مذكور في القرآن مخطوط في الصحف بين جميع الناس غير أنّ التركيّ للعلل التي ذكرناها أشدّ حنينًا وأكثر نزاعًا

وباب آخر ممّا كان يدعوهم إلى الرجوع قبل العزم الثاني والعادّة[1] المنقوضة ٨،٧
وذلك أنّ الترك قوم يشتدّ عليهم الحضر والحتوم[2] وطول اللبث والمكث وقلّة التصرّف والتحرّف وأصل بنيتهم إنّما وُضع على الحركة وليس للسكون فيهم نصيب وفي قوى أرواحهم فضل على قوى أبدانهم لأنّهم أصحاب توقّد وحرارة واشتعال وفطنة كثيرة خواطرهم سريع لحظهم وكانوا يرون الكفاية معجزة وطول المقام بلدة والراحة عقلة والقناعة من قصر الهمّة وأنّ ترك الغزو يورث الذلّة

وقد قالت العرب في مثل ذلك قال عبد الله بن وهب الراسبيّ حبّ الهوينا ٩،٧
يكسب النصب والعرب تقول من غلا دماغه في الصيف غلت قدره في الشتاء وقال أكثم بن صيفيّ ما أحبّ أنّي مكفيّ كلّ أمر الدنيا قيل ولم قال أخاف عادة العجز

فهذه كانت علل الترك في حبّ الرجوع والحنين إلى الوطن ومن أعظم ما كان ١٠،٧
يدعوهم إلى الشرود ويبعثهم على الرجوع ويكره عندهم المقام ما كانوا فيه من جهل قوّادهم بأقدارهم وقلّة معرفتهم بأخطارهم وإغفالهم موضع الردّ عليهم والانتفاع بهم ولأنّهم حين جعلوهم أسوة أجنادهم لم يقنعوا أن يكونوا في الحاشية والحشوة وفي غمار العامّة ومن عرض العساكر وأنفوا من ذلك[3] لأنفسهم

١ د: المادّة. ٢ الحضر والحتوم: د: الحصر. ٣ من ذلك: زيدت من د.

Qutaybah ibn Muslim, speaking of the Turks, observed, "They have a greater propensity to return to their homeland than a hobbled camel." Indeed, the camel experiences great longing for its home and familiar haunts. When in Oman, far away from Basra, it will run and plunge through every ravine to get to its native land over a route it has traveled only once before, relying on smells and scents and the successful application of the natural instinct particular to its kind, until finally it reaches its resting place, covering the whole distance separating Oman from Basra. This is why Qutaybah used the camel to illustrate his saying about the Turks. The Qur'an notes that a craving and fervent longing for the homeland is recorded as a feature of all humankind,[64] but for the reasons we have mentioned the Turk feels this longing and yearning most intensely. 7.7

There is another factor motivating their return home, even more than waning resolve and weakening habit[65]—namely, that the Turks find it very hard to endure enforced settlement, to stay permanently in one place, and to enjoy only limited freedom to move as they please. Their whole outlook is based on mobility; they have no interest in a sedentary life. Their souls exceed in strength their bodies, for they possess passion, enthusiasm, spiritedness, and acumen, being full of ideas and quick to comprehend. They regard it as impossible to be content with a bare subsistence, sheer stupidity to stay long in one place, a fetter on one's liberty to rest and take one's ease, a lack of ambition to be satisfied, and a cause of shame to give up raiding. 7.8

The Arabs have similar sayings. For example, ʿAbdallāh ibn Wahb al-Rāsibī said, "Love of leisure begets fatigue," and there is an Arab proverb: "He whose brain bubbles in summer, his pot will bubble in winter." And Aktham ibn Ṣayfī said, "I would not like to have enough of all the goods of the world," and when asked why, he replied, "I fear the habit of sloth." 7.9

These are the reasons why Turks love to return home and are nostalgic for their own country. However, one of the biggest factors that impels them to desert, provokes them to return home, and makes them averse to staying put is the situation they are placed in by their officers' ignorance of their capabilities, lack of acquaintance with their importance, and unfamiliarity with when to turn to them and make good use of them. Another factor is when the officers treat them on the same footing as the rest of the troops, for the Turks are not content to be in the rank and file, among the great undifferentiated mass of the army. They reject such an attitude with disdain and talk about what is due to 7.10

وذكروا ما يجب لهم ورأوا أنّ الضيم لا يليق بهم وأنّ الخمول لا يجوز عليهم وأنّهم في المقام على من لا يعرف حقّهم ألوم ممّن منعهم حقّهم

فلمّا صادفوا ملكًا حكيمًا وبأقدار الناس عليمًا لا يميل إلى سوء عادة ولا يجنح ١١،٧
إلى هوى ولا يتعصّب لبلد على بلد يدور مع التدبير حيثما دار ويقيم مع الحزم حيثما أقام أقاموا إقامة من قد فهم الحظّ ودان بالحقّ ونبذ العادة وآثر الحقيقة ووصل نفسه بقطيعة وطنه وآثر الإمامة على ملك الجبريّة[1] واختار الصواب على الإلف

ثمّ اعلم بعد هذا كلّه أنّ كلّ أمّة وقرن وكلّ جيل وبني أب وجدتهم قد برعوا ١٢،٧
في الصناعات وفضلوا الناس في البيان أو فاقوهم في الآداب وفي تأسيس الملك أو في النصر بالحرب فإنّك لا تجدهم في الغاية وفي أقصى النهاية إلّا أن يكون الله قد سخّرهم لذلك المعنى بالأسباب وقصرهم عليه بالعلل التي تقابل تلك الأمور وتصلح لتلك المعاني لأنّ من كان متقسّم الهوى مشترك الرأي متشعّب النفس غير موفّر على ذلك الشيء ولا مهيّأ له لم يحذق من تلك الأشياء شيئًا بأسره ولم يبلغ فيه غايته كأهل الصين في الصناعات واليونانيّين في الحكم والاداب والعرب فيما نحن فيه ذاكروه في موضعه وآل ساسان في الملك والأتراك في الحروب

ألا ترى أنّ اليونانيّين الذين نظروا في العلل لم يكونوا تجّارًا ولا صنّاعًا بأكفّهم ولا ١٣،٧
أصحاب زرع وفلاحة وبناء وغرس ولا أصحاب جمع ومنع وحرص[2] وكدّ وكانت الملوك تفرّغهم وتُجرى عليهم كفايتهم فنظروا حين نظروا بأنفس مجتمعة وقوّة وافرة وأذهان فارغة حتّى استخرجوا الآلات والأدوات والملاهي التي تكون جمامًا للنفس وراحة بعد الكدّ وسرورًا يداوي قرح المهموم فصنعوا من المرافق وصاغوا من المنافع كالقرسطونات والقبّانات والأسطرلابات وآلة الساعات وكالكونيا والكيران والبركار وكأصناف المزامير والمعازف والطبّ والحساب والهندسة

١ الإمامة على ملك الجبريّة: د: ملك الإقامة على ملك الحرّيّة. ٢ زيدت من د.

them. They regard ill-treatment as unbefitting, obscurity as unacceptable, and remaining with those who do not recognize their rights as more reprehensible than remaining with those who deny their claims.

Yet when Turks meet with a ruler who is perceptive and aware of people's true worth, with no inclination to evil practices or tendency toward arbitrary whims, showing no partiality for one country above another, governing with care and managing with prudence wherever he can, then they will settle down like those who understand their good fortune, submit to what is right, and cast aside their customary ways, opting for the path of justice and bringing themselves to accept severance from their homeland, judging the imamate preferable to despotic rule,[66] and choosing righteousness over natural habit. 7.11

Furthermore, you must understand that every people and era, every generation and lineage, will have a special aptitude in certain skills, whether they outperform the rest of humanity in eloquence, or surpass them in literary pursuits, in the founding of empire, or in military prowess. And you will find in the ultimate analysis that God has adapted and shaped them for that purpose by giving them the qualities and motivations appropriate and suitable for such attainments and objectives. For a person whose predilections, views, and ambitions are dissipated and scattered so that he does not devote his attention and effort to any one thing will not become skilled in any activity. Nor will he attain complete mastery of it, as the Chinese have done in handicrafts, the Greeks in philosophical learning and wise counsel, the Arabs in the fields described below, the Sasanians in statecraft, and the Turks in warfare. 7.12

Do you not see that the Greeks, who developed theories about causation, were never merchants or craftsmen, did not engage in agriculture or construction, and were unconcerned with amassing and preserving wealth and with struggle and toil? Rather, they were provided by their rulers with sufficient means to ensure they could be at leisure, and therefore they were able to engage in speculative thought with equanimity, an abundance of strength, and a carefree mind. As a result, they invented those tools, implements, and instruments that afford repose to the spirit, bring ease after labor, and generate delight to assuage the cares of the troubled. They fashioned and manufactured a number of convenient and useful devices, such as the Archimedean balance; the weighbridge; the astrolabe; the water clock; the carpenter's square; the blacksmith's bellows; the compass;[67] the various kinds of wind and stringed instruments; devices for medicine, arithmetic, geometry, and music; engines 7.13

واللحون وآلات الحرب كالمجانيق والعرّادات والرتيلات والدبّابات وآلة النفّاط وغير ذلك ممّا يطول ذكره وكانوا أصحاب حكمة ولم يكونوا فعلة يصوّرون الآلة ويخرطون الأداة ويصوغون المثال ولا يحسنون العمل به ويشيرون إليها ولا يمسّونها ويرغبون في التعليم ويرغبون عن العمل

١٤،٧ فأمّا سكّان الصين فإنّهم أصحاب السبك والصياغة والإفراغ والإذابة والأصباغ العجيبة وأصحاب الخرط والنجر والتصاوير والنسج والخطّ ورفق الكفّ في كلّ شيء يتولّونه ويعانونه وإن اختلف جوهره وتباينت صنعته وتفاوت ثمنه فاليونانيون يعرفون العلل ولا يباشرون العمل وسكّان الصين يباشرون العمل ولا يعرفون العلل لأنّ أولئك حكماء وهؤلاء فعلة

١٥،٧ وكذلك العرب لم يكونوا تجّارًا ولا صنّاعًا ولا أطبّاء ولا حسّابًا ولا أصحاب فلاحة فيكونوا مهنة ولا أصحاب زرع لخوفهم من صغار الجزية ولم يكونوا أصحاب جمع وكسب ولا أصحاب احتكار لما في أيديهم وطلب لما عند غيرهم ولا طلبوا المعاش من ألسنة الموازين ورؤوس المكاييل ولا عرفوا الدوانيق والقراريط ولم يفتقروا الفقر المدقع الذي يشغل عن المعرفة ولم يستغنوا الغناء الذي يورث البلدة والثروة التي تحدث الغرّة ولم يحتملوا ذلًّا قطّ فيميت قلوبهم ويصغّر عندهم أنفسهم

١٦،٧ وكانوا سكّان فياف وتربية العراء لا يعرفون الغمق ولا اللثق ولا البخار ولا الغلظ ولا العفن ولا التخم أذهان حديدة ونفوس منكرة فحين حملوا جدّهم ووجّهوا قواهم إلى قول الشعر وبلاغة المنطق وتشقيق اللغة وتصاريف الكلام وقيافة البشر بعد قيافة الأثر وحفظ النسب والاهتداء بالنجوم والاستدلال بالآثار وتعرّف الأنواء والبصر بالخيل والسلاح وآلة الحرب والحفظ لكلّ مسموع والاعتبار بكلّ محسوس وإحكام شأن المثالب والمناقب بلغوا في ذلك الغاية وحازوا كلّ أمنيّة وببعض هذه العلل صارت نفوسهم أكبر وهممهم أرفع وهم من جميع الأمم أفخر ولأيّامهم أذكر

of war such as the ballista, catapult, and siege towers and their rollers;[68] flame-throwers; and many others that it would take too long to mention. They were men of learning rather than deeds; they could draw a blueprint for a device or design an instrument and mold the prototype but were not skilled at using it. They could demonstrate how to make such things but could not operate them; they delighted in science but shied away from its application.

The inhabitants of China are men of the foundry and forge, molders and smelters, dyers of wondrous skill, joiners and carpenters, designers and weavers, calligraphers, and experts in working by hand everything they treat or handle, no matter how varied the material, the process, or the value. Thus, the Greeks understand causation but do not deal with application, whereas the Chinese deal with application and do not understand causation, for the former are philosophers and the latter practitioners. 7.14

Likewise, the Arabs have never been traders or craftsmen, doctors or mathematicians, agriculturalists—lest they be reviled—or peasants, because of their fear of the humiliation of paying the poll tax. They have never been devoted to the accumulation and acquisition of wealth, nor to hoarding their own possessions or pursuing what others possess. They have never sought to earn a living from the intricacies of weights and measures, and they know nothing of coins and carats. They have never suffered that crushing poverty that distracts from learning, nor experienced the wealth that begets insensitivity or the opulence that breeds folly. They have never tolerated an inferior status such as deadens their hearts or humiliates them in their own eyes. 7.15

Rather, they were desert dwellers brought up in the open, unfamiliar with a damp, humid habitat with its heavy vapors and unwholesome breath of decay,[69] possessing keen intellects and independent souls. When they apply all their energy and strength to poetry and eloquent speech; to sophisticated language and inflected discourse; to the investigation of humanity by scrutiny of its achievements;[70] to the preservation of tribal lineages; to navigating by the stars and drawing conclusions from their course and understanding their risings and settings;[71] to the inspection of horses, armor, and military equipment; to remembering what they have heard, heeding what they have experienced, and evaluating a person's good and bad qualities, then they excel in all these skills and attain all expectations. In some of these fields, their personal aspirations and ambitions have been greatly elevated so that they have become the proudest of all peoples and the most eager to memorialize their exploits. 7.16

وكذلك الترك أصحاب عمد وسكّان فياف وأرباب مواش وهم أعراب العجم كما أنّ هذيلاً أكراد العرب لم تشغلهم الصناعات ولا التجارات ولا الطبّ والفلاحة والهندسة ولا غراس ولا بنيان ولا شقّ أنهار ولا جناية[1] غلّات ولم يكن هممهم غير الغزو والغارة والصيد وركوب الخيل ومقارعة الأبطال وطلب الغنائم وتدويخ البلاد وكانت هممهم إلى ذلك مصروفة وكانت لهذه المعاني والأسباب مسخّرة ومقصورة عليها وموصولة بها أحكموا ذلك الأمر بأسره وأتوا على آخره وصار ذلك هو صناعتهم وتجارتهم ولذّتهم[2] وفخرهم وحديثهم وسمرهم فلما كانوا كذلك صاروا في الحرب كاليونانيّين في الحكمة وأهل الصين في الصناعات والأعراب فيما عددنا ونزّلنا وكآل ساسان في الملك والسياسة ١٧،٧

وممّا يستدلّ به على أنّهم قد استقصوا هذا الباب واستفرغوه وبلغوا أقصى غايته وتعرّفوه أنّ السيف إلى أن يتقلّده متقلّد أو يضربه ضارب قد مرّ على أيد كثيرة وعلى طبقات من الصنّاع كلّ واحد منهم لا يعمل عمل صاحبه ولا يحسنه ولا يدّعيه ولا يتكلّفه لأنّ الذي يذيب حديد السيف ويميعه ويصفّيه ويهذّبه غير الذي يمدّه ويمطله والذي يمدّه ويمطله غير الذي يطبعه ويسوّي متنه ويقيم خشيبته والذي يطبعه ويسوّي متنه سوى الذي يسقيه ويرهفه والذي يسقيه ويرهفه غير الذي يركّب قبيعته ويستوثق من سيلانه والذي يعمل مسامير السيلان وشاذَي القبيعة ونعل السيف غير الذي ينحت خشب غمده والذي ينحت خشب غمده غير الذي يدبغ جلده والذي يدبغ جلده[3] غير الذي يحلّيه والذي يحلّيه ويركّب نصله غير الذي يخرز حمائله وكذلك السرج وحالات السهم والجعبة والرمح وجميع السلاح ممّا هو جارح أو جُنّة والتركيّ يعمل هذا كلّه بنفسه من ابتدائه إلى غايته فلا يستعين برفيق ولا يفزع إلى رأي صديق ولا يختلف إلى صانع ولا يشغل قلبه بمطاله وتسويفه وأكاذيب مواعيده وبغرم كرائه ١٨،٧

---

١ ت، ق، د: جباية. ٢ ت، ق: (في الحرب) زيادة. ٣ والذي يدبغ جلده: زيدت من د.

Likewise, the Turks are tent dwellers, desert denizens, and owners of flocks. They are the Bedouin of the non-Arabs, just as the Hudhayl are the Kurds of the Arabs, in that they have nothing to do with manufacture, trade, medicine, agriculture, engineering, horticulture, building, cutting canals, or harvesting crops. They are exclusively interested in raids and incursions, hunting and horse riding, heroic combat and the quest for booty, and the subjugation of settled lands. They have no other ambitions; to these ideas and causes they are subordinated, constrained, and connected. They are masters in this and have attained perfection. This is their craft, their trade, their delight,[72] the subject of their boasts, conversation, and campsite stories. Hence, they are in war what the Greeks are in philosophy, the Chinese in handicrafts, the Bedouin Arabs in the ways we have enumerated above, and the Sasanians in government and statecraft. 7.17

One may infer from the following that the Turks have indeed made every effort to go deeply into the subject of warfare and achieved the most profound acquaintance of it. Before a sword is put on by its wearer or wielded by its bearer, it has passed through many hands and various kinds of craftsmen, none of whom can do another's work or excel in it, and indeed would not claim or even undertake to do so. For the man who smelts, purifies, and refines the metal of a sword is not the one who gives it shape; he is not the one who hammers it, making its body even and producing its natural form; and he is not the one who quenches and sharpens it. Another man fits its hilt and secures the tang;[73] the one who makes the rivets for the tang and for the cross guards[74] of the hilt and for the sword tip is not the one who carves the wood of the scabbard. He is different from the one who tans the leather for it, who in turn is not the one who decorates it; and the one who decorates it and fits its tip[75] is not the one who pierces the holes in the carrying straps. The same is the case with a saddle, the various stages in the manufacture of arrow and quiver, lance, or any other kind of armament, be it for attack or defense. Yet the Turk makes all the equipment himself from beginning to end, without the help of any partner or recourse to the opinion of any friend. He does not frequent a craftsman or fret about the latter's delays, procrastination, and false promises, or about the expense of hiring him. 7.18

١٩،٧ وحين بلغ أوس بن حجر صفة القانص وبلغ له الغاية في جمعه لأبواب الكفاية بنفسه قال

قَصِيٌّ مَبِيتِ ٱللَّيْلِ لِلصَّيْدِ مُطْعَمٌ   لِأَسْهُمِـهِ غَـارٍ وَبَارٍ وَرَاصِفُ[١]

وليس في الأرض كلّ تركيّ كما وصفنا كما أنّه ليس كلّ يونانيّ حكيمًا ولا كلّ صينيّ حاذقًا ولا كلّ أعرابيّ شاعرًا فائقًا ولكنّ هذه الأمور في هؤلاء أعمّ وأتمّ وفيهم أظهر وأكثر

٢٠،٧ قد قلنا في السبب الذي تكاملت به النجدة والفروسيّة في الترك دون جميع الأمم وفي العلل التي من أجلها نظّموا جميع معاني الحرب وهي معان تشتمل على مذاهب غريبة وخصال عجيبة فمنها ما يقضى لأهله بالكرم وببعد الهمّة وطلب الغاية ومنها ما يدلّ على الأدب السديد والرأي الأصيل والفطنة الثاقبة والبصيرة النافذة ألا ترى أنّه ليس بدّ لصاحب الحرب من الحلم والعلم والحزم والعزم والصبر والكتمان ومن الثقافة وقلّة الغفلة وكثرة التجربة ولا بدّ من البصر بالخيل والسلاح والخبرة بالرجال وبالبلاد والعلم بالمكان والزمان والمكايد وبما فيه صلاح الأمور كلّها

٢١،٧ والملك يحتاج إلى أواخ شداد وأسباب متان ومن أمتنها سببًا وأعمّها نفعًا ما ثبّته في نصابه وسكّنه في قراره وزاده في تمكينه وبهائه وقطع أسباب المطمعة فيه ومنع أيدي البغاة من الإشارة إليه فضلاً عن البسط عليه

٢٢،٧ قال ثمّ إنّ الترك عطفت على العرب بالمحاجّة والمقايسة وقالوا قلتم إن تكن القرابة ممّا يستحقّ بالكفاية فنحن أقدم في الطاعة والودّ والمناصحة وإن تكن تستحقّ بالقرابة فنحن أقرب قرابة قالوا والعرب بعد هذا صنفان عدنان وقحطان فأمّا القحطانيّ فنسبتنا إلى الخلفاء أقرب من نسبتهم ونحن أمسّ بهم رحمًا

١ وحين . . . وراصف: زيدت من د.

In a similar vein, Aws ibn Ḥajar describes the true hunter by expressing how he combines in one person all varieties of competence: 7.19

> Taking his night's repose in a remote spot, living off the game he catches,
> feathering, tipping, and splicing his own arrows.

Not every Turk on earth, however, fits our description, just as not every Greek is a philosopher, nor every Chinese a skilled artisan, nor every Bedouin Arab a superlative poet. Nevertheless, these qualities are very widespread and prominent among these peoples.

We have spoken of the reason the Turks specifically, and no one else, combine so perfectly military valor and horsemanship, and of how they command with such ease all aspects of warcraft, aspects that involve unique aptitudes and marvelous qualities. Some of these require those who possess them to have nobleness, far-reaching ambition, and perseverance, while others are indicative of apposite training, sound reasoning, and astute and penetrating understanding. Note that the warrior must also be endowed with self-control and knowledge, prudence and resolve, endurance and discretion, as well as training combined with vigilance and experience. He should also have a good eye for horse and weapon, plus experience of men and terrain, and knowledge of place, time, and stratagem, and of the smooth deployment of everything pertinent to them. 7.20

Government requires robust ties and firm bonds, and by far the strongest and most useful of these bonds is the one that sets it on a firm footing and ensures its stability, increases its power and prestige, removes opportunities for malefactors with evil designs upon it, and restrains the hands of rebels from even pointing in its direction, let alone drawing swords against it. 7.21

Then the Turks turned to the Arabs with the following reasoned argument. You Arabs say, "If closeness to the caliph is earned by dutiful behavior, then we deserve it, for we were the first to give him our obedience, affection, and good counsel. And if it is earned by kinship, then we also deserve it, for we are his nearest kin." However, the Arabs are not a uniform group but are of two stocks: ʿAdnānī and Qaḥṭānī. Now the relationship of us Turks to the caliphs is closer, and we are nearer in kinship, for the caliph is descended from Ishmael, son of Abraham, whereas Qaḥṭān and Eber are not part of that line. The 7.22

لأنّ الخليفة من ولد إسماعيل بن إبراهيم دون قحطان وعابر وولد إبراهيم عليه السلام إسماعيل وأمّه هاجر وهي قبطيّة وإسحاق وأمّه سارة وهي سريانيّة والستّة الباقون أمّهم قنطورا بنت مفطون عربيّة من العرب العاربة وفي قول القحطانيّة إن أمّنا أشرف في الحسب إذ كانت عربيّة وأربعة من الستّة هم الذين وقعوا بخراسان فأولدوا ترك خراسان فهذا قولنا للقحطانيّ وأمّا قولنا للعدنانيّ فإبراهيم أبونا وإسماعيل عمّنا وقرابتنا من إسماعيل كقرابتهم

٢٣،٧ قال الهيثم بن عديّ قيل لمبارك التركيّ وعنده حمّاد التركيّ إنكم من مذحج قال ومذحج هذا من هو ذاك وما نعرف إلّا إبراهيم خليل الله وأمير المؤمنين قال الهيثم وقد كان سقط إلى بلاد الترك رجل من مذحج فأنسل نسلاً كثيرًا ولذلك قال شاعر الشعوبيّة للعرب في قصيدة طويلة

زَعَمْتُمْ بِأَنَّ ٱلتُّرْكَ أَبْنَاءُ مَذْحِجٍ وَبَيْنَكُمُ قُـرْبَى وَبَيْنَ ٱلْبَرَابِـرِ
وَذٰلِكُمُ نَسْـلُ ٱبْنِ ضَبَّةَ بَاسِلٍ وَصُوفَانَ أَنْسَالُ كَثِيرُ ٱلْجَرَائِـرِ

وقال آخر

مَتَى كَانَتِ ٱلْأَتْـرَاكُ أَبْنَـاءَ مَذْحِجٍ أَلَا إِنَّ فِي ٱلدُّنْيَا عَجِيبًا لِمَنْ عَجِبْ

٢٤،٧ وقد سمعتم ما جاء في سدّ بني قنطورا وشأن خيولهم بنخل السواد وإنّما كان الحديث على وجه التهويل والتخويف بهم لجميع الناس فصاروا للإسلام مادّة جندًا كثيفًا وللخلفاء وقاية وموئلاً وجنّة حصينة وشعارًا دون الدثار

٢٥،٧ وفي المأثور من الخبر تاركوا الترك ما تاركوكم وهذه وصيّة لجميع العرب فإنّ الرأي متاركتنا ومسالمتنا وما ظنّكم بقوم لم يعرض لهم ذو القرنين وبقوله اتركوهم سمّوا الترك هذا بعد أن غلب على جميع الأرض غلبة وقسرًا وعنوة وقهرًا وقال

children of Abraham were Ishmael, whose mother was Hagar, an Egyptian; and Isaac, whose mother was Sarah, a Syrian; and six others, whose mother was Qeturah, daughter of Mafṭūn, one of the aboriginal Arabs.[76] The Qaḥṭānī tribes say, "Our ancestor has higher social prestige because she was an Arab." Now, four of the six children of Abraham by Qeturah settled in Khurasan and begot the Turks of Khurasan. This, therefore, is our reply to the Qaḥṭānī. To the ʿAdnānī, we say, "Abraham is our father and Ishmael is our cousin, and so our kinship to Ishmael is on par with theirs."

Al-Haytham ibn ʿAdī relates that Mubārak the Turk was told while in the company of Ḥammād the Turk, "You are of Madhḥij." He answered, "Who is this Madhḥij?[77] As ancestor we acknowledge only Abraham, friend of God and prince of believers." Al-Haytham goes on to say that a man of Madhḥij had ended up in the land of the Turks and sired numerous offspring, and for this reason a Shuʿūbī[78] poet said to the Arabs in the course of a long ode: 7.23

You assert that the Turks are sons of Madhḥij,
and that there is affinity between you and the Berbers,
But they are the sons of Ibn Ḍabbah, a hero,
while Ṣūfān are the descendants of a multitude of offenses.[79]

Another poet:

When were the Turks children of Madhḥij?
Indeed, the world contains marvels for those disposed to marvel.

You have heard the reports about the wall of the sons of Qeturah and their horsemen amid the palm trees of the Sawād, but it was only a story told to frighten and scare people by invoking their name.[80] In fact, they have become a mighty army that is a mainstay for Islam, and a protection, a refuge, and an impregnable defense for the caliphs, like a garment beneath the overcoat. 7.24

There is a saying reported on good authority, "Leave the Turks alone so long as they leave you alone." This is a recommendation to all the Arabs, for indeed it is best policy to leave us alone and keep peace with us.[81] Do you not think it apt for a people whom Alexander the Great did not dare attack that they should receive their name, Turks, by reason of his saying, "Let them alone."[82] Moreover, this occurred after he had decisively conquered the whole 7.25

عمر بن الخطّاب رضي الله عنه هذا عدوّ شديد طلبه[1] قليل سلبه فنهى كما ترى عن التعرّض لهم بأحسن كناية

والعرب إذا ضربت المثل في العداوة الشديدة قالوا ما هم إلّا الترك والديلم قال عملّس بن عقيل بن علّفة ٢٦،٧

تَبَدَّلْتُ مِنْهُ بَعْدَ مَا شَابَ مَفْرَقِي   عَدَاوَةَ تُرْكِيٍّ وَبُغْضَ أَبِي حِسْلِ

وأبو حسل هو الضبّ والعرب تقول هو أعقّ من ضبّ لأنّه يأكل أولاده

ولم يرعب قلوب أجناد العرب مثل الترك وقال خلف الأحمر ٢٧،٧

كَأَنِّي حِينَ أَرْهَنُهُمْ بَنِيَّ   دَفَعْتُهُمْ إِلَى صُهْبِ ٱلسِّبَالِ

قال وإيّاهم عنى أوس بن حجر

نَكَّبْتُهَا مَاءَهُمْ لَمَّا رَأَيْتَهُمْ   صُهْبَ ٱلسِّبَالِ بِأَيْدِيهِمْ بَيَازِيرُ

وحدّثني إبراهيم بن السنديّ مولى أمير المؤمنين وكان عالمًا بالدولة شديد الحبّ لأبناء الدعوة وكان يحوط مواليه ويحفظ أيّامهم ويدعو الناس إلى طاعتهم ويدرّسهم مناقبهم وكان فخم المعاني فخم الألفاظ لو قلت لسانه كان أردّ على هذا الملك من عشرة آلاف سيف شهير وسنان طرير لكان ذلك قولاً ومذهبًا قال حدّثني عبد الملك بن صالح عن أبيه صالح بن عليّ أنّ خاقان ملك الترك واقف مرّة الجنيد بن عبد الرحمن أمير خراسان وقد كان الجنيد هاله أمره وأفزعه شأنه وتعاظمه جموعه وجمعه وبعل به وبلغ منه ١،٨

---

١ د: كلبه.

world by force and compulsion. ʿUmar ibn al-Khaṭṭāb said, "This is an enemy hard to catch and yielding little booty." He therefore, as you can observe, strongly implied that he discouraged any engagement with them.

In this vein, when they coined a proverb for bitter enemies, the Arabs said, "They are nothing but Turks and Daylamis." And ʿAmallas ibn ʿAqīl ibn ʿUllafah said: 7.26

Once gray hairs appeared on the crown of my head, I received from him
the hostility of a Turk and the hatred of Abū Hisl.

Abū Hisl is the monitor lizard; the Arabs have a proverb, "More unnatural than a monitor lizard," because the latter eats its young.

Nobody ever struck such terror into the hearts of Arab troops as did the Turks. Khalaf al-Aḥmar said: 7.27

When I surrendered my sons to them as hostage,
it was as though I had handed them over to the men of ruddy mustaches.

And it was the Turks whom Aws ibn Ḥajar meant when he said:

I turned my camels away from their watering hole when I beheld them,
ruddy-mustached, with staves[83] in their hands.

Al-Junayd and the Khāqān and Sundry Other Reports

I was furnished with a report by Ibrāhīm ibn al-Sindī, Mawla of the caliph, a man well acquainted with our dynasty, extremely well disposed to those associated with our cause, a loyal servant to his patrons, who memorialized their great deeds, called for obedience to them, and impressed on people their fine qualities. He was so magnificent in thought and word that it would be truthful to say his tongue defended the state better than ten thousand drawn swords and keen lances. Now, he said that ʿAbd al-Malik ibn Ṣāliḥ informed him, on the authority of his father, Ṣāliḥ ibn ʿAlī, that Khāqān, the ruler of the Turks, once encamped by al-Junayd ibn ʿAbd al-Raḥmān, the governor of Khurasan. This greatly alarmed al-Junayd, who was awed by Khāqān's mustered troops; he did not know what to do and was at his wit's end. 8.1

وفطن به خاقان وعرف ما قد وقع فيه فأرسل إليه إنّي لم أقف هذا الموقف ٢،٨
وأمسك هذا الإمساك وأنا أريد مكروهًا فلا ترع ولو كنت أريد غلبة أو مكروهًا لقد كنت انتسفت عسكرك انتسافًا أعجلك فيه عن الرويّة وقد أبصرت موضع العورة ولولا أن تعرف هذه المكيدة فتعود بها على غيري من الأتراك لعرّفتك موضع الانتشار والخلل والخطأ في عسكرك وتعبيتك وقد بلغني أنّك رجل عاقل وأنّ لك شرفًا في بيتك وفضلاً في نفسك وعلمًا بدينك وقد أحببت أن أسأل عن شيء من أحكامكم لأعرف به مذهبكم فاخرج إليّ في خاصّتك لأخرج إليك وحدي وأسائلك عمّا أحتاج إليه بنفسي ولا تحتفل ولا تحترس فليس مثلي من غدر وليس مثلي يؤمن من نفسه ومن مكره وكيده ثمّ ينكث بوعده ونحن قوم لا نخدع بالعمل ولا نستحسن الخديعة إلّا في الحرب ولو استقام أمر الحرب بغير خديعة لما جوّزنا ذلك لأنفسنا

فأبى الجنيد أن يخرج إليه إلّا وحده ففصلا من الصفوف وقال سل عمّا ٣،٨
أحببت فإن كان عندي جواب أرضاه أجبتك وإلّا أشرت عليك بمن هو أبصر بذلك منّي قال ما حكمكم في الزاني قال الجنيد الزاني عندنا رجلان رجل دفعنا إليه امرأة تغنيه عن حرم الناس وتكفّه عن حرم الجيران ورجل لم نعطه ذلك ولم نخلّ بينه وبين أن يفعل ذلك لنفسه فأمّا الذي لا زوجة له فإنّا نجلده مائة جلدة ونحضّر ذلك الجماعة من الناس لنشهّره ونحذّره به ونعرّفه في البلدان لنزيد في شهرته وفي التحذير منه ولينزجر بذلك كلّ من كان يهمّ بمثل عمله فأمّا الذي قد أغنيناه فإنّا نرجمه بالجندل حتّى نقتله قال حسن جميل وتدبير كبير فما قولكم في الذي يقذف عفيفًا بالزنى قال يُجلد ثمانين جلدة ولا نقبل له شهادة ولا نصدّق له حديثًا

قال حسن جميل وتدبير كبير فما حكمكم في السارق قال السارق عندنا ٤،٨
رجلان رجل يحتال لما قد أحرزه الناس من أموالهم حتّى يأخذها بنقب حيطانهم

8.2 Khāqān, aware of this and realizing his state of mind, sent a message to him, saying, "I did not stop here and take this position because I wish a confrontation, so do not be alarmed. If I had desired victory, I could have scattered your army before you had time to think about it, since I have observed your weaknesses. And were it not that you might understand this tactic and employ it against other Turks, I would inform you of where your army is overstretched and where you have mistakenly left it vulnerable. I hear that you are an intelligent man, possessed of high honor in your family, personal merit, and knowledge of your religion. I therefore want to ask about some of your laws so that I may comprehend your code of conduct. Come out to me with just your personal entourage so that I may come out to you alone and ask you personally what I need to. But do not come surrounded by a large guard, for I am not one to play false; a person like me is not the sort to break his promise after he has given a pledge against guile or treachery. We are a people who do not practice deceit and approve of it only in war; and if war could be efficiently conducted without deceit, we would never permit ourselves to employ it."

8.3 Al-Junayd then insisted on coming out alone, so the two of them stood away from their armies, and al-Junayd said, "Ask what you want, and if I have an answer I consider satisfactory, I will impart it to you; if not, I will direct you to someone more expert in the matter." Khāqān then asked, "What is your judgment regarding a fornicator?" Al-Junayd answered, "In our view, a fornicator is one of two kinds: either a man on whom we have bestowed a wife to restrain him from resorting to the women of other men and his neighbors, or one to whom we did not grant a wife and to whom we have not allowed the opportunity of securing one for himself. The one who has no wife we flog with one hundred lashes, and that is done openly in the presence of the people so that we expose him and make a public example of him. We also broadcast his name throughout the realm to amplify his ill repute and our warning about him, and to deter anyone who has a mind to do as he has done. The one whom we had provided with a wife, we stone to death." Khāqān said, "Good, fine, an excellent plan. And what is your judgment regarding someone who falsely accuses a chaste person of adultery?" Al-Junayd replied, "We give him eighty lashes and do not thereafter accept his testimony or give legal credence to his statements."

8.4 "Good, fine, an excellent plan. And what is your judgment regarding a thief?" Al-Junayd answered, "In our view, a thief may be one of two kinds. There is the burglar who devises means to get at wealth that men have kept

وبالتسلّق من أعالي دورهم فهذا نقطع يده التي سرق بها ونقب بها واعتمد عليها ورجل آخر يخيف السبيل ويقطع الطريق ويكابر على الأموال ويشهر السلاح فإنّ منعه صاحب المتاع قتله فهذا نقتله ونصلبه على المناهج والطرق قال حسن جميل وتدبير كبير قال فما حكمكم في الغاصب والمستلب قال كلّ ما فيه الشبهة ويجوز فيه الغلط والوجوه كالغصب والاستلاب والجناية والسرقة لما يؤكل أو يُشرب فإنّا لا نقطع فيما فيه شبهة ونتمحّل لذلك وجهًا غير السرقة

٥،٨ قال حسن جميل وتدبير كبير قال فما حكمكم في القاتل وقاطع الأذن والأنف قال النفس بالنفس والعين بالعين والأنف بالأنف وإن قتل رجلاً عشرة قتلناهم ونقتل القوي البدن بالضعيف البدن وكذلك اليد والرجل

٦،٨ قال حسن جميل وتدبير كبير قال فما تقولون في الكذّاب والنمّام والضرّاط قال عندنا فيهم الإقصاء لهم وإبعادهم وإهانتهم ولا نقبل شهادتهم ولا نصدّق أحكامهم قال وليس إلّا هذا قال هذا جوابنا على ديننا قال له أمّا النمّام عندي هو الذي يضرّب بين الناس فإنّي أحبسه في مكان لا يرى فيه أحدًا وأمّا الضرّاط فإنّي أكوي استه وأعاقب ذلك المكان فيه وأمّا الكذّاب فإنّي أقطع الجارحة التي بها يكذب كما قطعتم اليد التي بها يسرق وأمّا الذي يضحك الناس ويعوّدهم السخف فإنّي أخرجه من سلطاني وأصلح بإخراجه عقول رعيّتي

٧،٨ قال فقال الجنيد بن عبد الرحمن أنتم قوم تردّون أحكامكم إلى جواز العقول وإلى ما يحسن في ظاهر الرأي ونحن قوم نتّبع الأنبياء ونرى أن لم نصلح على تدبير العباد وذلك أنّ الله تعالى أعلم بغيب المصالح وسرّ الأمر وحقائقه ومحصوله وعواقبه والناس لا يعلمون ولا يرون الحزم إلّا على ظاهر الأمور وكم من مضيع يسلم وحازم يعطب قال ما قلت كلامًا أشرف من هذا ولقد ألقيت لي فكرًا طويلاً

safe, by breaking through their walls or climbing over their housetops; we cut off the hand he stole with, broke in with, or depended upon. The second kind makes the highway dangerous by robbery, seeking to seize property with a show of weaponry and killing the owner of the goods if he resists. Such a one we execute by crucifixion at the wayside." "Good, fine, an excellent plan. And what is your judgment regarding the petty thief and the pilferer?" Al-Junayd replied, "In any instance where doubt or mistake is possible, or where there are kinds of minor appropriation like larceny, pilfering, purloining, and the theft of food or drink, we do not cut off the hand if there is any doubt or the possibility of construing the act as other than theft."

"Good, fine, an excellent plan. And what is your judgment regarding a mur- 8.5
derer or one who cuts off an ear or a nose?" Al-Junayd responded, "A life for a life, an eye for an eye, a nose for a nose. If ten men jointly commit a murder, we put them all to death. We execute the strong man in recompense for a weak victim, and likewise with a hand or foot."

"Good, fine, an excellent plan. And what do you say about a liar, scandal- 8.6
monger, or frequent farter?" Al-Junayd rejoined, "In their case, our custom is to banish them from society and hold them in contempt; we do not accept their testimony nor validate their decisions." "Is that all?" said Khāqān. "This is our answer according to our religion," responded al-Junayd. "In my opinion," declared Khāqān, "the scandalmonger is a person who sows discord among people, so I confine him in a place where he can see nobody. I brand the frequent farter in the anus, thus punishing the pertinent part of him. With the liar, I cut off the offending member by which he spread falsehood, just as you cut off the hand of the one who steals. I expel from my dominion the one who makes people laugh and reduces them to folly, and I thereby safeguard the good sense of my subjects."

Thereupon, al-Junayd ibn ʿAbd al-Raḥmān remarked, "You are a people 8.7
who relate your rules to the sanction of reason and to that which is approved by obvious good sense, but we are a people who follow the prophets and think that it is not right for us to regulate the faithful. That is because God is most knowledgeable about the hidden and secret nature of their best interests, its truths and consequences, whereas humans only understand and perceive the prudent course in a superficial way. Many a lost person finds safety and many a cautious person goes to ruin." "You have never said a nobler word than this," said Khāqān, "and you have given me a lot to think about."

قال إبراهيم قال عبد الملك قال صالح قال الجنيد فلم أر أوفى ولا أنصف ولا أفهم ٨،٨
ولا أذكى منه ولقد واقفته ثلاث ساعات من النهار وما تحرّك منه شيء إلّا لسانه وما منّي شيء لم أحرّكه وهكذا يصفون ملوك الترك يزعمون أنّ ساسان وخاقان الأكبر تواقفا ببعض الكسور وفصلا من الصفّين وطالت المناجاة فلمّا انفتلا قالوا كان خاقان أركن وآدب وكان مركب كسرى أركن وآدب ولم يتحرّك من خاقان إلّا لسانه وكان برذونه يرفع قائمة ويضع أخرى وكان مركب كسرى كأنّما صُبّ صبًّا وكان كسرى يحرّك رأسه ويشير بيده

قالوا ومن الأعاجيب أنّ الحارث بن كعب لا يقوم لحزم وحزم لا تقوم لكندة ٩،٨
وكندة لا تقوم للحارث بن كعب قالوا ومثل ذلك من الأعاجيب في الحارث أنّ العرب لا تقوم للترك والترك لا تقوم للروم والروم لا تقوم للعرب

قال جهم بن صفوان الترمذيّ قد عرفنا ما كان بين فارس والترك من الحرب ١٠،٨
حتّى تزوّج كسرى أبرويز خاتون بنت خاقان يستميله بذلك الصهر ويدفع بأسه عنه وقد عرفنا الحروب التي كانت بين فارس والروم وكيف تساجلوا الظفر وبأيّ سبب غُرس الزيتون بالمدائن وسوسا وبأيّ سبب بُنيت الروميّة ولِمَ سُمّيت بذلك ولم بنى كسرى على الخليج قبالة قسطنطينية النواويس وبيوت النار ولكن متى ظهرت الروم على ترك خراسان ظهورًا متواليًا ضربوا بها المثل إلى آخر دار مسه ومن هناك من الأشباه ومن يتخلّل هذا النسب

وكانت خاتون بنت خاقان عند أبرويز فولدت له شيرويه وقد ملك شيرويه ١١،٨
بعد أبرويز فتزوّج شيرويه مريم بنت قيصر فولدت له فيروزًا بنته[١] هي أمّ يزيد الناقص بن الوليد وكان يقول ولدني أربعة أملاك كسرى وخاقان وقيصر ومروان وكان يرتجز في حروبه التي قتل فيها الوليد بن يزيد بن عاتكة

أَنَا ٱبْنُ كِسْرَى وَأَبِي خَاقَانْ   وَقَيْصَرٌ جَدِّي وَجَدِّي مَرْوَانْ

[١] د: بنتا.

Ibrāhīm concluded ʿAbd al-Malik's report from Ṣāliḥ by noting al-Junayd's comment, "I have never met someone more trustworthy, just, understanding, and intelligent. I stood before him for three hours of the day and he moved not a limb save his tongue, whereas I was gesticulating with my whole body." The rulers of the Turks are commonly described as being like this. For example, it is said that Khosrow of the House of[84] Sāsān and Khāqān the Great once met on a bridge.[85] They stood apart from their respective armies and had a long confidential conversation. When they parted, it was reported that Khāqān was the steadier and better trained of the two while Khosrow's mount was the steadier and better trained of their horses. No part of Khāqān moved except his tongue, while his horse restlessly pawed the ground. Khosrow's mount was as if forged from metal, while Khosrow nodded his head and gesticulated with his hand. 8.8

They say it is an astonishing thing that al-Ḥārith ibn Kaʿb cannot stand up to Ḥazm, nor Ḥazm to Kindah, nor Kindah to al-Ḥārith ibn Kaʿb,[86] and it is equally astonishing that in war the Arabs cannot stand up to the Turks, nor the Turks to the Romans, nor the Romans to the Arabs. 8.9

Jahm ibn Ṣafwān al-Tirmidhī is the authority for what follows. We all know how a state of war existed between the Persians and Turks until Khosrow Parwīz[87] married Khāqān's daughter, Khātūn, seeking to conciliate Khāqān by this alliance and to deflect his military might. We also know of the wars that took place between the Persians and Romans and how they contested the victory in turn, and why olive trees were planted at Ctesiphon and Susa, why Constantinople was built and why it was given that name, and why on the strait opposite Constantinople Khosrow built mausoleums and fire temples. But when did the Romans ever triumph over the Turks of Khurasan with a series of victories, for the like of which the Turks have become proverbial to the ends of the realm of the Masah and those like them who had become their kin.[88] 8.10

Khātūn, daughter of Khāqān, was the wife of Parwīz and bore to him Shiroi, who succeeded Parwīz on the throne and married Maryam, daughter of Caesar.[89] She bore to him Peroz, whose daughter[90] was the mother of Yazīd the Deficient, son of al-Walīd, who used to say, "Four kings were among my forefathers: Khosrow, Khāqān, Caesar, and Marwān." He would recite this line in connection with the wars in which al-Walīd ibn Yazīd ibn ʿĀtikah was killed:[91] 8.11

I am a scion of Khosrow; Khāqān is my ancestor,
While Caesar and Marwān are my forefathers.

فلمّا صار إلى الافتخار في شعره بالنجدة والثقافة بالحرب لم يفخر إلّا بخاقان فقط فقال ١٢،٨

فَإِنْ كُنْتُ أَرْمِي مُقْبِلاً ثُمَّ مُدْبِرًا وَأَطْلَعُ مِنْ طَوْدٍ زَلِيقٍ عَلَى مُهْرِ
فَخَاقَانُ جَدِّي فَٱعْرِفِي ذَاكَ وَٱذْكُرِي أَخَايِرُهُ فِي ٱلسَّهْلِ وَٱلْجَبَلِ ٱلْوَعْرِ

قوله وأطلع يريد وأنزل وهي لغة أهل الشام وأخذوها من نازلة العرب في أوّل الدهر وجعل دابّته مهرًا لأنّ ذلك أشدّ وأشقّ

وقال الفضل بن العباس بن رزين أتانا ذات يوم فرسان من الترك فلم يبق أحد ممّن كان خارجًا إلّا دخل حصنه وأغلق بابه وأحاطوا بحصن من تلك الحصون وأبصر فارس منهم شيخًا يطلع إليهم من فوق فقال له التركيّ لئن لم تنزل إليّ لأقتلنّك قتلة ما قتلتها أحدًا قال فنزل إليه وفتح له الباب ودخلوا الحصن واكتسحوا كلّ شيء فيه فضحك من نزوله إليه وفتحه له وهو في أحصن موضع وأمنع مكان ١٣،٨

ثمّ أقبل به إلى حصن أنا فيه فقال اشتروه منّي قلنا لا حاجة لنا في ذلك قال فإنّي أبيعه بدرهم واحد فرمينا إليه بدرهم فخلّى سبيله ثمّ أدبر عنّا ومضى مع أصحابه فما لبث إلّا قليلاً حتّى عاد إلينا فوقف حيث نسمع كلامه فراعنا ذلك فأخرج الدرهم من فمه وكسره بنصفين وقال لا يسوى درهمًا وهذا غبن فاحش فخذوا هذا النصف وهو على كلّ حال غال جدًّا بالنصف الآخر قال فإذا هو أظرف الخلق قال وكنّا نعرف ذلك الرجل بالجبن وقد كان سمع باحتيال الترك في دخول المدن وعبور الأنهار في الحروب فتوهّم أنّه لم يتوعّد بفتح الباب ١٤،٨

وقال ثمامة ما شبّهت الذرّ إلّا بالترك لأنّ كلّ ذرّة على حدتها معها من المعرفة بادّخار الطعم ومن الشمّ والاسترواح وبجنب المدّخر حتّى لا يبيت إلّا في جحره ثمّ الاحتيال للناس في الاحتيال لها بالصمامة والعفاص والمزدجر وتعليق الطعام على الأوتاد والبرّادات مثل الذرّ مع صاحبتها ١٥،٨

However, when Yazīd came to boast in his poetry about bravery and skill in war, he boasted only of Khāqān: 8.12

I can shoot facing forward or backward,
and mount a colt from a slippery height
because Khāqān was my ancestor; mark this and remember it
—I can outdo him on smooth ground or rugged mountains.

The word "I mount" here has the sense of "I descend," a Syrian dialectal usage that they adopted from Arab settlers in the earliest period. He makes his mount a colt because this is a more spirited and difficult animal.[92]

Al-Faḍl ibn al-ʿAbbās ibn Razīn told the following story. Some Turkish horsemen descended upon us one day, and everyone who had set out retreated into his tower house[93] and barred the door. The Turks surrounded one of those houses, and one of them saw an old man looking out at them from above. The Turk said, "Unless you come down to me, I will kill you in a way I have never killed anyone before." So the old man came down and opened the door, and they entered the house and seized everything in it. The Turk laughed at the fact that the old man would come down and open the door when he was fortified in an impregnable position. 8.13

He brought the old man along to the tower I was in and said, "Buy him from me," to which we replied, "We have no need of him." "I will sell him for a single dirham." So we threw him a dirham and he let the old man go. Then the Turk left and went off with his companions. A little later he returned and stood within earshot, which greatly alarmed us. He took the dirham out of his mouth[94] and broke it in two, saying, "He is not worth a dirham, it would be daylight robbery; take back this half. He is very expensive as it is, even for the other half." An extremely witty fellow indeed! We knew that the old man was a coward. He had heard how cunning Turks were at entering towns and crossing streams in war, so he imagined that the Turk would not have issued empty threats over the opening of a door. 8.14

Thumāmah asserts that ants are just like Turks, for every individual ant has some knowledge of how to store food, how to smell and sniff out things, and how to put aside gathered provisions[95] so that it may return safely at night to the anthill. It also has a capacity for outwitting humans in their ploys against ants—namely, for sealing and corking food in containers, employing deterrent measures, and securing food with pegs or in coolers. Like the ant with its comrades, so also the Turks have an instinct for cooperation. 8.15

وقال أبو موسى الأشعريّ كلّ جنس يحتاج إلى أمير ورئيس ومدبّر حتّى الذرّ ١٦،٨
وروى أبو عمرو الضرير أنّ رئيس الذرّ الرائد الذي يخرج أوّلاً لشيء قد شمّه دون أصحابه لخصوصيّة خصّه الله تعالى بها ولطافة الحسّ فإذا حاول حمله وتعاطى نقله وأعجزه ذلك بعد أن يبلي عذرًا أتاهنّ فأخبرهنّ فرجع وخرجت بعده كأنّها خيط أسود ممدود وليست ذرّة أبدًا تستقبل ذرّة أخرى إلّا واقفتها وسارتها بشيء ثمّ انصرفت عنها وكذلك الأتراك كلّ واحد منهم غير عاجز عن معرفة مصلحة أمره إلّا أنّ التفاضل واجب في جميع أصناف الأشياء والنبات والموات وقد تختلف الجواهر وكلّها كريم وتتفاضل العتاق وكلّها جواد

وقد قلنا في مناقب جميع الأصناف بجمل ما انتهى إلينا وبلغه علمنا فإن وقع ذلك ١،٩
بالموافقة فبتوفيق من الله تعالى وصنعه عزّ ذكره وإن قصر دون ذلك فالذي قصر بنا نقصان علمنا وقلّة حفظنا وأسماعنا فأمّا حسن النيّة والذي نضمر من المحبّة والاجتهاد في القربة فإنّا لا نرجع في ذلك إلى أنفسنا بلائمة وبين التقصير من جهة التفريط والتضييع وبين التقصير من جهة العجز وضعف القوّة فرق

ولو كان هذا الكتاب من كتب المناقضات وكتب المسائل والجوابات وكان ٢،٩
كلّ صنف من هذه الأصناف يريد الاستقصاء على صاحبه ويكون غايته إظهار فضل[١] نفسه وإن لم يصل إلى ذلك إلّا بإظهار نقص أخيه ووليّه لكان كتابنا كبيرًا كثير الورق عظيمًا ولكان العدد الذين يقضون لمؤلّفه بالعلم والاتّساع في المعرفة أكثر وأظهر[٢] ولكنّا رأينا أنّ[٣] القليل الذي يجمع خير من الكثير الذي يفرق ونحن نعوذ بالله من هذا المذهب ونسأله العون والتسديد إنّه سميع قريب فعّال لما يريد

١ زيدت من د. ٢ ولكان العدد . . . وأظهر: زيدت من د. ٣ رأينا أنّ: زيدت من د.

Abū Mūsā l-Ashʿarī notes that every species needs a leader to direct and organize affairs, even ants, while Abū ʿAmr al-Ḍarīr[96] relates that the chief of the ants is the scout, who goes out first on account of something that he alone has smelled, and not his fellows, because of a special ability that God Almighty has allotted to him and because of his sensory sensitivity. When he has attempted to carry it and struggled to transport it but finds himself unable to do so even after trying every trick, he goes back and tells the others. Then he returns and they come out behind him like a single long black thread. No ant ever meets another without confronting it and confiding something to it before parting. The same goes for the Turks. Every one of them can understand what is best for his own situation, but competition is a necessary feature of all things, whether animate or inanimate. Jewels differ greatly, though all are valuable, and thoroughbred horses vie with one another for precedence, though all are fine steeds. 8.16

Conclusion

We have now stated the qualities of all the groups in the caliphal army by bringing together everything we heard and learned about them. If this meets with approval, it is by the aid and agency of God Almighty, cherished be His remembrance. If we fail, it is due to the deficiency of our knowledge and the paucity of our recollection and hearing. So far as good intention goes, and the fond endeavor that is concealed in our heart, we cannot attach any blame to ourselves. There is a difference between a shortcoming due to remissness and carelessness, and a shortcoming due to limited ability and capacity. 9.1

If this book had been concerned with disputations, or with questions and answers, and had each protagonist wanted to produce an exhaustive refutation of their counterpart, and had his objective been the demonstration of his own excellence even at the expense of showing up the failings of brother or patron, this would have been an enormously bulky book, and the number of those crediting its author with knowledge and wide learning would have been much greater and more apparent. However, I thought something small that unites is better than something big that creates dissension. We seek refuge in God from the latter, and we ask Him for help and guidance. He is all-hearing, close at hand, able to do as He wills. 9.2

Notes

1 In this preface, al-Jāḥiẓ uses the terms Imam (*imām*), Caliph (*khalīfa*), and Sultan (*sulṭān*) interchangeably; for simplicity, I will translate them all by the term Ruler. Note that *sulṭān* is also used impersonally, with the sense of "sovereignty" or "authority."

2 The former is automatic and obligatory whereas the latter is earned through merit and voluntary action. The two Arabic terms used here have legal connotations: *dhimām* (synonym: *dhimmah*) refers to a contract that guarantees security of life and property, and *kifāyah* alludes to a duty (*farḍ*) that is fulfilled when performed by a sufficient number of people (the classic example is jihad to protect the lands of Islam, which does not necessitate the participation of the whole of a society, but an adequate portion of it).

3 For the nature and significance of these five groups of the army, see the translator's Introduction and the Glossary.

4 D has "Meccan and Medinan." The pairs of groups given in the rest of this section are likely meant to be regarded as belonging to Arabia.

5 Again, D stresses the Arabian connection, speaking of "the lowlanders and uplands of the tribe of Ṭayy" and noting the saying "Hudhayl are the Kurds of the Arabs," an allusion to the Hudhayl tribe's homeland of the mountains around Mecca, in the same way that the Kurds inhabited the mountains of Iran and Iraq.

6 "Problematic lineage" amalgamates three specialist terms that appear in the Arabic text: *muʿalhaj*, "born of a free father and a slave mother"; *mudharraʿ*, "having a mother more noble than the father"; and *muzallaj*, "of suspect origin or lineage."

7 The implication is that a shared environment unites the southern (Qaḥṭānī) and northern (ʿAdnānī) Arab groups just as it unites the Turks and Khurasanis, and it is not disrupted by differences in lineage and ethnicity.

8 Ar. Kisrā. This is presumably an allusion to the fact that the Lakhmid Arab chief al-Nuʿmān refused to marry his daughter to the Sasanian Emperor Khosrow II.

9 These widespread sayings of the Prophet are found in the earliest collections of such material; see, for example, Ibn Abī Shayba, *al-Muṣannaf*, 4:308 (#20472), 7:368 (#36761).

10 This is a quotation of a verse either by al-Aʿwar ibn Yazīd al-Kilābī or by Yazīd ibn Ṣuḥār according to Hārūn in his edition of al-Jāḥiẓ's *al-Burṣān wa-l-ʿurjān*, where this verse is also quoted (p. 465). Both bodily features are typically regarded as desirable, suggestive of pride/honor and strength/endurance respectively.

11 The fact that al-Jāḥiẓ lists this with prized objects suggests that he is referring to kaolin, which was used to make porcelain in China from ca. AD 600 and entered Middle Eastern markets around AD 800.

12 The two main terms in this sentence, *nuqabā'* and *nujabā'*, can simply mean "leaders" and "nobles" respectively, but since the key actors in the revolution that brought the Abbasid family to power acquired hallowed status, they bear an ideological flavor in this context.

13 The "trenches" refers to a battle between the Umayyad governor Naṣr ibn Sayyār and the pro-Abbasid Khurasani soldiers (see al-Ṭabarī, *Ta'rīkh al-rusul wa-l-mulūk*, 2.1935, and also §3.8 below). The second term, *kfyh*, is uncertain; I suggest translating it as "sandy tract," thinking of the term *kuffah*.

14 Defective dotting of letters means my translation is conjectural. Harley Walker reads: *minnā al-mustakhbiyah wa-man yumarrikh al-nīmiyyah*, translating: "To us belong those that make tents of camel's hair, and that discharge far arrows of the nim-tree."

15 Again, defective dotting obscures the reading. Khazzān and al-Jawzatayn are probably corruptions of names of places where two major victories were won by the Abbasid revolutionary army; D has Ḥarrān, which is a city in northern Syria, but it surrendered to the Abbasids without a fight.

16 These two terms are Persian. The first pertains to *zaghand*, "the roaring of beasts of prey," and the second to *āzādmard*, "free man," which has connotations of chivalry.

17 Their hair is long like that of a woman, because they promise not to cut it before achieving victory, and their clothes are like those of a monk, because they disdain worldly adornments.

18 All Abbasid caliphs were descended from Muḥammad ibn 'Alī, and al-Mutawakkil, who was reigning in al-Jāḥiẓ's day, was indeed the tenth Abbasid caliph.

19 That is, by the so-called 'Uthmāniyyah, who held that the murder of the third caliph, 'Uthmān, was unjust, and that his successor, 'Alī, was not a legitimate caliph. Most were pro-Umayyad and anti-Abbasid.

20 These are the names of private militias that fought on behalf of the Umayyads against the Abbasids; see Athamina, "Non-Arab Regiments," 368–71.

21 These four ancient peoples (see the entries in the Glossary) are not specifically known to be strong, but it is a common medieval belief that ancient peoples were bigger and stronger.

22 D has *Zābaj*, a kingdom centered on modern Java. However, the Zanj are better known in Arabic sources and feature often in al-Jāḥiẓ's writings; they serve here to add another remote location to the list: the far south.

23 This is a reference to the siege of the Kaaba in Mecca during the second Arab civil war (64–72/683–92).

24 Persian: *bāzfikand*, or *bāzafkan*, which signifies a piece of cloth worn on the upper back part of the armor to protect the neck.

25 A compound word made from Arabic *kāfir* (infidel) and Persian *koba* (implement for crushing or pounding), possibly some sort of traditional Iranian weapon, since it was used by many Iranian rebels against Umayyad rule.

26 Instead of "Iraqi or Hijazi," D has *ʿarnabah*, which van Vloten emends to *gharībah*, yielding the translation "Any rare/abstruse art . . ."; one could also emend to *ʿarabiyyah*: "Any Arab art . . ."

27 Specifically, "wheeling round to attack" (*al-mujāwalah wa-l-mushāwalah*) and "returning after retreating" (*al-karr wa-l-farr*).

28 Tag and hockey are my suggestions for *dabbūq* (described by lexicographers simply as a well-known children's game) and *ṭabṭāb* (described as a ball game played with a *ṭabṭābah*, "wooden bat or mallet").

29 Specifically, a bird or animal fixed to the ground (*mujaththamah*), a target on a spear (using the Persian word *burgāsb*), and a bird in flight (*ṭāʾir khāṭif*).

30 Ar. *sajjāʿ*, which literally means someone who can speak in rhymed prose (*sajʿ*), the expected medium for the utterances of an Arabian diviner.

31 The first seven men were among the twelve leaders of the Abbasid revolutionary council; Mālik ibn al-Ṭawwāf was an Abbasid missionary. See Agha, *The Revolution Which Toppled the Umayyads*, 308–13 (nos. 1, 3–4, 8, 10–12 on his table of *nuqabāʾ*), 359. The last four men named belonged to the clan of Imruʾ al-Qays of the tribe of Tamīm, as explicitly stated by Ṭabarī (*Taʾrīkh*, 2:1988); the clan's name should be written as al-Maraʾī, though in the manuscripts it is written as al-Murrānī or al-Mazānī.

32 Specifically, paternal uncles and cousins, which may be relevant to the Abbasid-Alid rivalry, the former emphasizing paternal ties and the latter, given the descent of their imams from the Prophet's daughter, maternal ties.

33 Agha, *The Revolution Which Toppled the Umayyads*, 308–13 (nos. 2 and 5–7 on his table of *nuqabāʾ*).

34 Ar. *khuʾūlah*, literally signifies relationship of a maternal uncle (and maternal aunt).

35 These four groups appear in al-Jāḥiẓ's *Book of Misers*; Serjeant identifies them as rebel groups known as tough urban fighters (*Book of Misers*, 41n194), which makes sense given that the Banawis were very much a Baghdad-based army and had to defend the city when it was besieged by al-Maʾmūn.

36 Literally "tools and implements," but the ensuing list suggests physical objects are not what is meant. Al-Jāḥiẓ does not go on to talk about the talents and abilities of "each of

the groups" as he claims here, which is one of many hints that either he made multiple drafts of this epistle or had different intentions for its contents.

37 Ar. *shākiriyyah* and *jund*. The former is a term of Turco-Persian origin referring to private militias assembled by a ruler and tied to him by personal bonds, and the latter is just the standard word for the army or a regiment thereof.

38 Literally "he opened up his uvula to."

39 For an insightful discussion of this and related passages, see Agha, "Language as a Component of Arab Identity in al-Jāḥiẓ."

40 Literally "with respect to lawsuits and blood money."

41 Whereas the other examples in this section are of people whose relationships may be accepted even though biologically fictive, this case is the opposite: Zayd and ʿAmr's relationship can be denied even though biologically real. The names Zayd and ʿAmr are used here by way of example (like saying A and B) rather than in reference to historical figures.

42 Q Aḥzāb 33:6 says that «his wives are their mothers», and the copy of the Qur'an held by Ubayy ibn Kaʿb allegedly continued: "and he is father to them." «The religion of Abraham your father» is a reference to Q Ḥajj 22:78.

43 The three categories are, as Harley Walker neatly translates it, a wet-nurse, a stepmother, and a foster father. The reference to the Qur'an perhaps concerns Q Nūr 24:61, which says that there is nothing wrong with eating in the homes of your paternal and maternal uncles.

44 It "makes good sense" because ʿAdnānī tribes were allegedly descended from Ishmael son of Abraham, and Quraysh, the tribe of the Prophet Muḥammad, was reckoned as belonging to them.

45 Literally "crumbs and meat on a trestle." The first word appears in T as *nathar*, which can mean anything scattered or in small pieces, but as *bsw* in D, which van Vloten and others have read as *bi-sūʾ* ("in a bad way"). The second phrase, "meat on a trestle," is a proverbial metaphor for defenselessness.

46 Or, less likely, "too fast for the latter to deliberate," reading *rawiyyah* rather than *ruʾyah* (sight).

47 That is, so that their horses still had plenty of energy for the battle. In this clause and in other places in this section, the author sometimes uses the feminine singular, thinking of the Kharijites as a collective, and sometimes the masculine plural, thinking of them as individuals.

48 T and Q have "excites love" (*ḥabbabat*), which does not fit the sense of this paragraph, so I emend to *jannabat*. D has "rips out" (*khalaʿ*) their hearts, which seems excessive unless it is intended metaphorically.

49 Ar. *al-ḥukmu lillah*, literally "judgment belongs to God," a slogan of the early Kharijites.

50 Literally "fill its gaps," because at a full gallop the space between the fore and hind legs will be repeatedly narrowed.

51 D has "to the order" (*li-l-amr*), which does not fit well here, but the sentence is likely corrupt, and the original sense may well have been that the Turk trained his horse to turn only when given the order to do so.

52 The words in italics in this sentence are all well-known commands to the respective animals. For the horse, D gives *aqdim*, "go forward," whereas T has *ajdhim*, "speed up," which is a rarer word and so is perhaps preferable.

53 Ar. *naḥḥās*; strictly, this is a coppersmith rather than, as one would expect, an iron-smith; Hārūn emends to *nakhkhās*, "trader (in horses and cattle)."

54 That is, because he has been sitting on a horse for so long.

55 D's "Yamāmī" is more likely than T's "Yemeni," as the first five items in this list refer to regions where the Kharijites were very active (and the next four items are Kharijite sects), which is true of Yamāmah (in eastern Arabia) but not of Yemen.

56 Cupping is the placing on the body of special cups to create suction and thereby increase blood flow to an affected area and promote healing. Its practitioners, cuppers, were often regarded with disdain, perhaps because they worked with bodies and their fluids.

57 The words for reward and threat here, *al-waʿd* and *al-waʿīd*, have religious connotations—namely, divine forgiveness and divine retribution—and feature in the Muʿtazilite doctrine that God's promise to reward the righteous and requite sinners cannot be reversed by later intercession.

58 Ar. *sujūn*, literally "prisons"; or one could emend to *shujūn*, "steep valley roads."

59 Ar. *dūna l-jibāl*, literally "just short of the mountains"; the city of Ḥulwān is in the Zagros Mountains. The point is that they keep to the Iranian side of the range and do not generally cross over to the Iraqi side.

60 That is, because in that case the Turks would have surpassed anyone else in these fields; the reference to the Basrans' wisdom is perhaps a playful boast on the part of al-Jāḥiẓ, a Basran himself.

61 It is implied at the end of §6.10 that the testimony of Thumāmah has ended and, since no other informant is named, one assumes that al-Jāḥiẓ is now speaking.

62 Ar. *nash'uhā*; van Vloten emends to *nasharahā*, "He spread them/let them spread," which is possible, but al-Jāḥiẓ perhaps wanted to use the same root as appears in the upcoming Qur'anic verse (see next note).

63 The Qur'anic verse cited, Q Wāqiʿah 56:35, is referring to wives or houris, but al-Jāḥiẓ is using it to support his contention that all persons are created the same, and it is their environment that shapes them.

64 The Qur'an does not specifically refer to love of one's homeland, but it does say that «God made the earth for you as a place to settle» (Q Ghāfir 40:64) and frequently mentions the misfortune of those who are forced from their homes (*diyār*).

65 That is, the resolve and habit that kept them in Iraq might weaken and make them yield to their desire for their homeland. Van Vloten emends *thānī* to *thābit* and accepts D's reading of *al-mādda* instead of T's *al-ʿāda*, which gives, as Harley Walker translates it, "steadfast purpose and exhausted resources," but one expects two parallel expressions.

66 D has "preferring the realm of settled life over the realm of freedom," which would work as a restatement of the previous ideas, though the version in T could be seen as a subtle indication of support for the Abbasid government.

67 The first and third of these three instruments are clear: A *kūniyā* (from Greek *gōnia*) is a set square for drawing right angles and a *birkār* is a compass or dividers for drawing circles. The second item, *kīrān*, is unclear; I have read it as the plural of *kūr* (or *kīr*), meaning furnace or bellows, but it is only a suggestion, and it is likely that the word has been corrupted (D has *shīzān*, which signifies objects made from a type of Indian wood, especially bowls).

68 Ar. *rutayla*, "scorpion," is probably a calque translation of Greek *phalangion*, also meaning "scorpion" but with a special technical sense in the plural of "rollers for moving heavy objects," here the rolling platform for the *dabbābāt*, "siege towers."

69 The contrast is between the dry air of the Arabian plateau and the humid climate of Iraq.

70 Ar. *qiyāfat al-athar*. This phrase can refer to the art of following a person's tracks/footprints, but more likely it refers here to study of the monuments and works of art that humans have left behind.

71 Ar. *al-anwāʾ*. Books on this topic offered weather-forecasting tips for farmers based on the position of the sun and stars.

72 T and Q add "in war," but I think this is an accidental copying of the same phrase from the following sentence, and so I have omitted it from the Arabic text.

73 *Qabīʿah* often means the pommel of a sword, but here it likely stands for the whole handle (hilt), which is otherwise not mentioned. The "tang" of a sword is the part at the top of the blade that slides into the hilt.

74 Van Vloten suggests without explanation *shāribay al-qabīʿah*, "the two moustaches of the hilt," presumably thinking of the curved shape of some sword cross guards (also called quillons).

75 Presumably the chape (reinforced metal foot) of the scabbard.

76 Qeturah, a wife or concubine of Abraham in his later years, had six sons by him (Genesis 25:1–2), who are usually regarded as having Arab/Arabian connections, especially Midian. In Arabic sources, she is usually assigned an Arab mother; Ibn Saʿd (d. 230/845)

names her as Maqṭūr, almost identical in form to Mafṭūn, and he also has some of her sons settle in Khurasan (*al-Ṭabaqāt al-kubrā*, 1.40), so this Arab spin on biblical genealogy probably predates al-Jāḥiẓ.

77 Ṭabarī, *Ta'rīkh al-rusul wa-l-mulūk*, 2.276–80 (Ḥammād), 555, 560–63 (Mubārak). Madhḥij probably stands for the southern (Qaḥṭānī) Arabs in general here; Mubārak clearly considers the Turks to be one with the northern ('Adnānī) Arabs as descendants of Abraham, presumably via Qeturah and not Hagar.

78 That is, one who supported a cosmopolitan, less Arab-centric type of Islam. See Savran, *Arabs and Iranians in the Islamic Conquest Narrative*, ch. 2, and Ibn Qutaybah, *The Excellence of the Arabs*, Introduction.

79 The people of Ṣūfān were allegedly formed from many tribes, serving at the Kaaba in Mecca, and their mongrel origins are probably what is being alluded to here.

80 This seems to be a blend of two stories that link the sons of Qeturah to legendary narratives. One concerns the wall erected by Alexander the Great to keep out the barbarian hordes of the Central Asian steppe, and the other is an apocalyptic narrative that recounts how the descendants of Qeturah burst forth from Khurasan and descended on southern Iraq in such large numbers that every palm tree was used as a hitching post for their horses, and they threatened to expel all the inhabitants unless they were given land for themselves (e.g., Ibn Ḥammād, *Kitāb al-Fitan*, 2:674–83).

81 Note the switch to the first person, implying the Turks are the subject.

82 The Arabic verb here, *utrukū*, contains within it the word *Turk*, though it is of course just a play on words and not a genuine etymology for Turk.

83 D has *mārīn*, which one could take as an alternative plural of *mārin* (rather than the usual *mawārin*), meaning "a supple spear," but van Vloten and Hārūn opt for *bayāzīr*, "staves," because it is the word used in the official collection of Aws's poems and it fits the rhyme.

84 The text only has "Sasan," but this is just the name of a ruling dynasty of the Iranian empire, not one individual, so I add "Khosrow of the House of" to complete the sense; Khosrow I is meant.

85 Ar. *ba'ḍ al-kusūr*. Hārūn notes that *kusūr* can mean "the windings of valleys and mountains," but that would be a difficult meeting place. Van Vloten emends to *ba'ḍ al-jusūr*, "one of the bridges," which is plausible; or one might argue, given that *jisr* is a loanword from Syriac *geshrā*, "bridge," that *kisr* was an alternative form of *jisr*.

86 These three names refer to tribal groups of southern Arabia.

87 It is Khosrow (I) Anūshirwān, not Khosrow (II) Parwīz, who is usually thought to have married the daughter of a Central Asian ruler, possibly Hephthalite.

88 This last section is obscure. The most problematic word is *d'rmsh*; I have translated it as two words, the first being *dār*, "realm," but it could be a single toponym; Harley Walker writes "Darmisa" without explanation.

89 Syriac, Arabic, and Persian—but not Greek—Christian sources say that Khosrow married Maryam (Maria), daughter of the Byzantine Emperor Maurice (d. AD 602), and begat Shiroi. Elite Zoroastrians are allowed, even sometimes encouraged, to marry their immediate family members, so Shiroi could have married Maryam after Khosrow's death, but it is more likely that al-Jāḥiẓ or his source is confused.

90 I have made a minimal amendment (*bintā hiyya* to *bintuhu hiyya*) to make the text grammatically correct, but I think some words are missing and originally there was a reference to Shāh-i Āfrīd, who was a daughter of Peroz (a son of Yazdagird III, not of Shiroi). See Ṭabarī, who cites the same line of poetry (*Ta'rīkh al-rusul wa-l-mulūk*, 2:1874).

91 Yazīd (III) ibn al-Walīd killed his cousin al-Walīd (II) ibn Yazīd in 126/743. The Caesar mentioned in the poem is Heraclius, and Marwān is Caliph Marwān I, who was Yazīd III's grandfather.

92 This passage looks like a gloss on the poem, whether by al-Jāḥiẓ himself or a later copyist, which at some point became incorporated into the main text.

93 Ar. *ḥiṣn*, which means any sort of reinforced structure, from a fortress to a fortified dwelling; the latter is meant here, perhaps with only upper windows to limit access.

94 That is, where he had stored it, apparently a common practice in the medieval world.

95 Ar. *janb al-muddakhar*; van Vloten emends to *tajannub al-muzjir*, "avoidance of that which scares away (i.e., dangers)," and Hārūn reads *najb al-muddakhar*, "husking the gathered provisions." Neither significantly improves the text as it is, though it is true that the text may be corrupt here.

96 Hārūn (*Rasā'il al-Jāḥiẓ*, 1:85n4) notes that this person is mentioned in other works of al-Jāḥiẓ; he is perhaps to be identified with a religious scholar of Basra of that name, who transmitted from several well-known experts in Islamic law of the second half of the second/eighth century.

Glossary

ʿAbbād ibn al-Ḥuṣayn (d. ca. 65/685) famous general and horseman of the tribe of Tamīm who was in charge of the security force (*shurṭah*) at Basra for Ibn al-Zubayr.

Abbasids second dynasty of the Islamic Empire, which came to power by ousting the Umayyad dynasty in a revolution in 132/750.

ʿAbd al-Malik ibn Ṣāliḥ (d. 196/812) son of the Abbasid Ṣāliḥ ibn ʿAlī, a general for the Caliph Hārūn al-Rashīd and one-time governor of Mosul.

ʿAbd Shams son of ʿAbd Manāf; he and his brother Hāshim, allegedly conjoined twins separated at birth, were the forefathers of the first two ruling dynasties of Islam, the Umayyads and the Abbasids, respectively.

ʿAbdallāh ibn Wahb al-Rāsibī (d. 38/658) a leader of the early Kharijites, who fought at the Battle of Ṣiffin in 37/657 and was killed the following year at the Battle of Nahrawān in central Iraq.

ʿAbd al-Muṭṭalib (d. ca. AD 578) son of Hāshim ibn ʿAbd Manāf, whose descendants constitute the clan of Hāshim, to which belong the Prophet Muḥammad, the ʿAlids, and the Abbasids.

al-ʿAbdī (d. ca. 20/640) Jārūd ibn al-Muʿallā, a Christian Arab poet of the tribe of ʿAbd al-Qays of eastern Arabia, who converted to Islam at the end of the life of the Prophet Muḥammad.

Abraham portrayed in the Bible as the founding father of the special relationship between God and the Jews; he is also a key figure in Christianity and Islam, who establishes "the House" (understood as the Kaaba in Mecca) with his son Ishmael.

Abū ʿAbd al-Ḥamīd Qaḥṭabah ibn Shabīb al-Ṭāʾī (d. 132/749) chief of the Abbasid revolutionary forces in Khurasan, who led them westward in 130/748 and on to victory against the Umayyad armies.

Abū Anasah (d. ca. 12/633) or Anasah, a Mawla of the Prophet who served as his gatekeeper; some say he was martyred at the Battle of Badr, but more often it is said he died during the caliphate of Abū Bakr.

Abū l-Baṭṭ (fl. 200/816) Aḥmad ibn ʿAmr al-Dhuhlī, an Abbasid general who fought in several campaigns during the reign of al-Maʾmūn.

Abū l-Ḥakam ʿĪsā ibn Aʿyan (fl. 120s/740s) of the tribe of Khuzāʿah, one of the twelve revolutionary leaders of the Abbasid movement.

Abū Ḥamzah ʿAmr ibn Aʿyan (fl. 120s/730s) of the tribe of Khuzāʿah, one of the twelve revolutionary leaders of the Abbasid movement.

Abū Manṣūr (fl. 120s/740s) Ṭalḥah ibn Zurayq, of the tribe of Khuzāʿah, one of the twelve revolutionary leaders of the Abbasid movement.

Abū Mūsā l-Ashʿarī (d. ca. 48/668) ʿAbdallāh ibn Qays, Companion of the Prophet who played a major role in the Islamic conquests and was governor at different times of Kufa and Basra for the caliphs ʿUmar and ʿUthmān.

Abū Muslim ʿAbd al-Raḥmān ibn Muslim (d. 137/755) principal architect of the Abbasid revolution, probably from eastern Iran, who organized and directed the movement until its success in 132/750, though he was murdered on the orders of Caliph al-Manṣūr.

Abū Najm (fl. 120s/740s) ʿImrān ibn Ismāʿīl, of the clan of Abū l-Muʿayṭ, one of the twelve revolutionary leaders of the Abbasid movement.

Abū Salamah Ḥafṣ ibn Sulaymān (d. 132/750) allegedly a freed slave from Kufa, who became the chief Abbasid missionary in Iraq, but was murdered that same year on the orders of the Caliph al-Ṣaffāḥ.

Abū Shujāʿ Shabīb ibn Bukhārākhudā al-Balkhī not known to our sources, but two elements of the name suggest a member of the Central Asian elite: Bukhārākhudā, which means "lord of Bukhara," and al-Balkhī, which means a native or long-time resident of Balkh in modern northern Afghanistan.

Abū Sufyān (d. ca. 33/653) son of Ḥarb ibn Umayya, forefather of the Sufyanid branch of the Umayyad dynasty and father of Muʿāwiyah I, the first Sufyanid caliph.

Abū Zubayd al-Ṭāʾī (d. 62/682) al-Mundhir ibn Ḥarmalah, a Christian Arab poet who was born in the pre-Islamic period and enjoyed the favor of the rightly guided caliphs ʿUmar and ʿUthmān.

ʿĀd ancient Arabian tribe mentioned often in the Qurʾan, which notes their construction of monumental buildings and the destruction of those buildings by a violent wind sent by God.

ʿAdnān the founding father of the northern Arabs according to Muslim genealogists.

al-Akhnas ibn Shurayq (fl. AD 610s) influential member of the western Arabian tribe of Thaqīf; he is mentioned as an opponent of the Prophet Muḥammad in the latter's biography and as the object of certain Qur'anic verses against slander and calumny (Q Qalam 68:10–13).

Aktham ibn Sayfī (d. 44/664) an orator and arbitrator of the tribe of Tamīm, famous for his proverbs and pithy wisdom.

ʿAlī ibn Abī Ṭālib (d. 40/660) cousin and son-in-law of the Prophet Muḥammad and regarded as the fourth rightly guided caliph; a rival of the future Caliph Muʿāwiyah in the first Arab civil war.

ʿAlī ibn ʿAbdallāh grandson of al-ʿAbbās ibn ʿAbd al-Muṭṭalib, an uncle of the Prophet Muḥammad.

ʿAmallas ibn ʿAqīl ibn ʿUllafah poet of the tribe of Murrah in the Umayyad period who visited the caliphal court in Damascus with his father.

Amelikites referred to in the Bible as a nomadic people who lived in the deserts of Sinai and northwestern Arabia and who were the enemies of Israel.

ʿĀmir ibn Ḍubārah (d. 131/749) senior Umayyad general who had much success fighting Kharijites in Iraq and Iran; he fell in battle against the Abbasid revolutionary forces.

Amorium ancient city of west central Anatolia, about 150 miles (250 kilometers) southwest of modern Ankara, Turkey; it was seized from the Byzantines by the Caliph al-Muʿtaṣim in August 838, which was regarded as a great triumph and celebrated in prose and verse.

Arab al-Jāḥiẓ uses this term to designate a distinct people who were united by a common language (Arabic), culture, and homeland (Arabia).

Aws a major tribe of Medina during the lifetime of the Prophet Muḥammad; they had been adversaries of another important Medinan tribe, the Khazraj, but the two were reconciled and became key supporters (*anṣār*) of the Prophet Muḥammad.

Aws ibn Ḥajar sixth-century Arabian poet, of the tribe of Tamīm, who had close links with the court of the Lakhmid kings of al-Ḥīrah in southern Iraq.

Azraqī member of the Kharijite subsect known as the Azāriqah, regarded as the most fanatical of the Kharijites.

Balkh River or Balkh-ab; it arises in the lakes of Bamiyan province in the Hindu Kush, then flows west and north before terminating in irrigation canals around the city of Balkh in modern north Afghanistan.

Banawis or *abnāʾ* (*al-dawla*), "sons (of the regime)," a term for the offspring of those Khurasanis who had fought in the Abbasid revolution; they mostly settled in Iraq and were loyal to the new government. See the translator's Introduction.

Bashshār (d. 168/784) ibn Burd, a poet of Persian ancestry, who grew up in Basra, then moved to Baghdad and became an important figure at the court of Caliph al-Mahdī.

Bedouin inhabitants of the arid regions (*badw*) of the Middle East; the collective term for them in the Qur'an and pre-Islamic Arabian inscriptions is *aʿrāb*, which is also used by al-Jāḥiẓ, who categorizes them as Arabs.

Canaanites residents of the land of Canaan, a region of the southern Levant that flourished in the second half of the second millennium BC, associated in the Bible with the "promised land."

al-Ḍabbī (d. ca. 183/780) al-Mufaḍḍal ibn Muḥammad, an important collector of poetry and traditions about Arabian history and author of a famous verse anthology.

Daylamis inhabitants of Daylam, a mountainous region of northwest Iran, near the southwest coast of the Caspian Sea; they were well known for their martial abilities and provided troops for both the Sasanian and Islamic Empires.

Dhū l-Yamīnayn Ṭāhir ibn al-Ḥusayn (d. 207/822) commander of al-Ma'mūn's forces in the civil war with his brother al-Amīn (r. 193–97/809–13) and subsequently al-Ma'mūn's governor in Khurasan.

Ḍirār ibn al-Azwar al-Asadī (d. ca. 18/639) famous warrior of the early Arab Muslim conquests and a companion of the Prophet Muḥammad; he is thought to have died in Syria from the plague.

Eber great-grandson of Shem, son of Noah; in the Bible he has two sons: Yoktan, identified by Muslim genealogists with Qaḥṭān, ancestor of the southern Arabs, and Peleg, from whom Ishmael, son of Abraham, was descended, and so also ʿAdnān, ancestor of the northern Arabs.

Emigrants (Ar. *muhājirūn*) the supporters of the Prophet Muḥammad in Mecca who then "emigrated" (*hājara*) with him from Mecca to Medina in 1/622.

al-Faḍl ibn al-ʿAbbās ibn Razīn of the tribe of Sulaym; his father is said to have known Mālik ibn Dīnar, a scholar and preacher of Basra who died around 130/748, which suggests that al-Faḍl flourished in the early Abbasid period.

al-Faḍl ibn Sahl (d. 202/818) convert from Zoroastrianism to Islam at the hands of al-Ma'mūn who rose to become the chief advisor and vizier of his patron before being assassinated by rivals for the caliph's favor.

Farghānah ancient kingdom between the River Jaxartes (modern Syr Darya) and the Tien Shan mountains, later incorporated into the Muslim province of Transoxiana, now a region straddling the borderlands of modern eastern Uzbekistan and southwestern Kyrgyzstan.

Gog and Magog two peoples portrayed in Christian and Muslim legend as numberless barbarian hordes, who were shut up behind walls in the Central Asian mountains by Alexander the Great.

Ḥabashī a member of an East African ethnic group, subject to the king of Axum (in modern northern Ethiopia) in the early centuries AD; the collective term is Ḥabashat, from which is derived the Latin word *Abyssinia*.

Ḥammād the Turk (fl. 140s/760s) a personal servant of the Caliph al-Manṣūr and a source of many anecdotes about him in Muslim historical sources.

Ḥamzah ibn Adrak (d. 213/828) Kharijite leader of eastern Iranian origin who spearheaded a long-running rebellion in Khurasan that began in 179/795 and continued until his death.

al-Ḥarīsh ibn Hilāl (d. 82/701) famous general and poet of the tribe of Tamīm who fought in many campaigns in Khurasan in the late first/seventh century.

Ḥarūrī one of several terms used to refer to members of the Kharijite sect of Islam; the name is explained as a reference to the first Kharijites, who withdrew from the army of the fourth caliph, ʿAlī ibn Abī Ṭālib, to the village of Ḥarūrā' near Kufa in southern Iraq.

Hāshim (d. ca. AD 500) ibn ʿAbd Manāf, great-grandfather of the Prophet Muḥammad and forefather of the Hashimite clan of the tribe of Quraysh.

Hawāzin Arabian tribe found in central west Arabia, especially in the steppe between Mecca and Medina.

al-Haytham ibn ʿAdī (d. 207/822) Kufan scholar who was a major transmitter of historical narratives, genealogies, and poetry.

Helpers (Ar. *anṣār*) the Medinans, chiefly of the tribes of Aws and Khazraj, who supported the Prophet Muḥammad and the Emigrants who came with him from Mecca.

Hijaz region comprising most of the west coast of Arabia, including the coastal strip along the Red Sea and the mountain range that runs alongside it from Jordan to Mecca.

Ḥimyarite member of a kingdom that ruled southern Arabia ca. AD 280–530; its incorporation into the Islamic Empire in the seventh century meant the gradual loss of its pre-Islamic language and identity in favor of Arabic and Arabness.

Ḥumayd ibn ʿAbd al-Ḥamīd (d. 210/826) senior Abbasid general from the Khurasani city of Ṭus, who fought in the civil war between al-Amīn and al-Maʾmūn on behalf of the latter.

Ibāḍī member of a moderate Kharijite subsect known as the Ibāḍiyyah, based chiefly in southern Iraq, northwestern Africa, and eastern Arabia.

Ibn Ḍabbah ʿAbdallāh ibn Yazīd, of the tribe of Thaqīf in western Arabia; his maternal aunt's relatives knew the Prophet and his sons fought in the Arab conquests in far-flung places, including Africa.

Ibn Ḍubārah see ʿĀmir ibn Ḍubārah.

Ibn Hubayrah (d. 132/750) Yazīd by name, a prominent general commended for his military skill; he was the last Umayyad governor of Iraq and long held out against the Abbasid revolutionary armies.

Ibn Judayʿ al-Kirmānī (d. 130/748) either ʿAlī or ʿUthmān, who were both sons of Judayʿ al-Kirmānī, a senior Umayyad general active in Khurasan and Transoxiana, and who were both killed by Abū Muslim's forces in the same year.

Ibn al-Zubayr (d. 73/692) ʿAbdallāh, a contender for the caliphate during the second Arab civil war; he belonged to the Asad clan of Quraysh and was the nephew of the Prophet Muḥammad's wife ʿĀʾishah.

Ibrāhīm ibn al-Sindī (fl. early third/ninth century) an Abbasid courtier like his father before him and a Mawla of al-Maʾmūn; he was very knowledgeable about Abbasid history and an important informant of al-Jāḥiẓ.

Ikhshīd al-Ṣughdī not known to our sources, but the elements of the name suggest a member of the Central Asian elite: *ikhshīd* is a Central Asian royal title and al-Ṣughdī is an ethnonym referring to Sogdians of Transoxiana.

imam refers either to a prayer leader, a religious leader, or the caliph; comes from the Arabic verb *amma*, to be at the front of or to lead the way.

Isaac the son of Abraham by his wife Sarah and putative ancestor of the twelve tribes of Israel; his name is written in Arabic as Isḥāq.

Ishmael the son of Abraham by his maidservant Hagar and putative ancestor of the northern Arabs; his name is written in Arabic as Ismaʿīl.

Jabalī a resident of the province of the Jibāl, located in the west of Iran in the Zagros Mountains.

Jahm ibn Ṣafwān al-Tirmidhī (d. 128/746) Muslim theologian of the Umayyad period, born in Iraq but then moved to Khurasan, where he served as a propagandist for the rebel al-Ḥārith ibn Surayj.

Jazarī a resident of the province of Jazīrah.

Jazīrah the Arabic name, literally meaning "island," for the region of North Mesopotamia, which lies in modern northern Iraq and southeastern Turkey and is bounded by the Euphrates and Tigris rivers.

Jumʿat al-Īyādiyyah said to be another name for Hind bint al-Khass (or the name of her sister), a woman of the pre-Islamic period famous for her rhetoric and wisdom.

al-Junayd ibn ʿAbd al-Raḥmān (fl. early second/eighth century) Umayyad governor of Khurasan, who led many campaigns against the Turks in Transoxiana.

Khalaf al-Aḥmar (d. ca. 180/796) famous transmitter of Arabic poetry; his parents were prisoners of war from Farghānah in Transoxiana who had been brought to Iraq, where Khalaf grew up.

Khālid ibn ʿUrfuṭah (d. 60s/680s) a member of the tribal confederation of Quḍāʿah and an ally of the Qurashī clan of Zuhrah; he was a Companion of the Prophet and a general in the early Arab Muslim conquests.

Khāqān (or *khāgān*, later *khān*) title of rulers of various medieval Turkic kingdoms in Central Asia; in this epistle, it is used as a personal name for Suluk, who ruled the Turgesh confederation and fought the Arabs in Transoxiana until his death in 120/738.

Khāqān the Great probably Ishtemi (r. AD 552–75), ruler of the Western Turkic Khaganate, who made an alliance with Khosrow I to fight the Hephthalites.

Kharijite member of a major Islamic sect that began as a mutiny against the fourth caliph, ʿAlī ibn Abī Ṭālib, for negotiating with Muʿāwiyah, who succeeded as the fifth caliph; they believed that the best person should be caliph, whatever their tribal or ethnic identity, and that serious wrongdoers forfeited their membership of the Muslim community and should be killed.

Khātūn the title of the queen of a Turkic ruler, used as a personal name in this epistle.

Khazraj a major tribe of Medina during the lifetime of the Prophet Muḥammad; they had been adversaries of another important Medinan tribe, the Aws, but the two were reconciled and became key supporters (*anṣār*) of the Prophet.

Khosrow (I) (r. AD 531–79) ruler of the Sasanian Persian Empire, famous for enacting wide-ranging social and economic reforms and for his wise governance.

Khosrow (II) (r. AD 602–28) bore the regnal name Parwīz ("victorious"); ruler of the Sasanian Persian Empire, who waged an ultimately unsuccessful war against the Roman Empire from AD 603 until his death.

Khurasani a resident of the eastern Iranian province of Khurasan; more particularly, a member of the army based in Khurasan that fought against the Umayyad dynasty in the revolution of ca. 132/750 and brought to power the Abbasid dynasty.

Madhḥij a large southern Arabian "Qaḥṭānī" tribe, mentioned in pre-Islamic Arabian inscriptions.

Maghribī a resident of the province of the Maghrib, northwestern Africa.

al-Ma'mūn (r. 197–218/813–33) seventh Abbasid caliph, famous for his love of knowledge and classical learning.

al-Manṣūr (r. 136–58/754–75) second Abbasid caliph and founder of the city of Baghdad.

Marwān (I) (d. 65/685) fourth Umayyad caliph, who reigned for just one year, succeeded by his sons and close relatives until the rise of the Abbasids.

Marwān (II) (r. 127–32/744–50) grandson of Marwān I and the fourteenth Umayyad caliph; he spent most of his reign fighting various rebels, in particular the Kharijites and the Abbasid revolutionaries.

Maryam or Maria; mentioned in Syriac, Arabic, and Persian—but not Greek—sources as the daughter of Emperor Maurice (d. AD 602) and wife of Khosrow II.

Mawla a term either for a freedman—that is, a slave or prisoner of war manumitted in return for certain benefits to the manumitter—or for a client, someone who has become bound by mutual agreement to a patron. See the translator's Introduction.

Mubārak the Turk (fl. 160s/780s) a general of the Caliph al-Hādī, who helped suppress a Zaydi Shi'ite rebellion outside Mecca in 179/786.

al-Muhallab ibn Abī Ṣufrah (d. 83/702) an Arab general of the tribe of Azd, who fought in numerous wars from the 20s/640s until his death and held many governorships, notably of Khurasan.

Muḥammad ibn 'Alī (d. 126/744) great-grandson of al-'Abbās ibn 'Abd al-Muṭṭalib, uncle of the Prophet Muḥammad, and the founding father of the Abbasid dynasty.

Muḥammad ibn al-Ashʿath (d. 149/766) of the tribe of Khuzāʿah; governor of Khurasan for Abū Muslim and of Damascus and then Egypt for Caliph al-Manṣūr, who also sent him to Ifrīqiyah (the Maghrib) to retake Qayrawān from Kharijite rebels.

Muḥammad ibn al-Jahm (fl. late second/eighth century) client of the powerful Barmakid family, who were of eastern Iranian origin and who served as secretaries and courtiers of the early Abbasid caliphs until their sudden fall from grace in 187/803.

Mūsā ibn Kaʿb (d. 141/758) of the tribe of Tamīm; one of the twelve leaders in the Abbasid revolutionary council and a general. He was made governor of the Jazīrah and was sent on a mission to overthrow the last Umayyad governor of Sind.

Mu'tah site of a battle that took place between the Byzantines and Muslims in the year 8/629 in modern east central Jordan; it is famous for being the first battle the Muslims fought outside of Arabia.

al-Muʿtaṣim (billāh) (r. 218–27/833–42) eighth Abbasid caliph, usually credited with the innovation of using Turks in the caliphal army.

Muṭīʿ ibn Iyās al-Laythī (d. 169/785) poet who spent time at the court of al-Manṣūr and al-Mahdī.

al-Nābighah (d. ca. AD 604) the nickname of Ziyād ibn Muʿāwiyah al-Dhubyānī, a famous pre-Islamic poet who frequented the courts of the Ghassanids and Lakhmids, the imperial Arab allies of Byzantium and Persia, respectively.

Najdī member of the Kharijite subsect known as the Najdiyyah, based chiefly in central and eastern Arabia.

Naṣr ibn Sayyār (d. 131/748) Arab general who fought in many campaigns in Transoxiana; he was the last Umayyad governor of Khurasan, in which post he died opposing the Abbasid revolutionary forces.

Nubātah ibn Ḥanẓalah (d. 130/748) a senior Umayyad general, governor of Ahwāz and later of Jurjān in northern Iran; he was killed fighting Abbasid revolutionary forces.

Oxus the ancient name of the modern Amu Darya, a large river of Central Asia; it separated Khurasan from the region to the east, called Transoxiana by the Romans and simply "what is beyond the river" (*mā warāʾ al-nahr*) by the Arabs.

Peroz (b. 15/636) son of Yazdagird III, the last Persian emperor; after his father's death, he fled to China and lived in exile.

Qaḥṭān the founding father of the southern Arabs according to Muslim genealogists, who identified him with the biblical Yoktan, son of Eber.

al-Qāsim ibn Sayyār (fl. early third/ninth century) Abbasid scribe and poet who lived in Baghdad during the reign of al-Ma'mūn.

al-Qāṭūl a settlement on the River Tigris, about 90 miles (145 kilometers) north of Baghdad, established by the Caliph Hārūn al-Rashīd and visited by the Caliph al-Muʿtaṣim in his search for a place to house his Turkish troops before opting for nearby Samarra.

Qays a confederation of Arabian tribes that originated in the low-lying areas of the Tihāmah in southwestern Arabia, but by the time of the Prophet Muḥammad they had spread much farther to the east and north of Arabia.

Qeturah (Ar. Qanṭūrā) a concubine or wife of Abraham in his later years, by whom he had six sons according to Genesis 25:1–2; she is given an Arab mother in Muslim tradition.

Quraysh the western Arabian tribe to which the Prophet Muḥammad and all caliphs belonged.

Qutaybah ibn Muslim (d. 96/705) general who spearheaded the Muslim conquests in Transoxiana during the reign of the Caliph al-Walīd (r. 86–96/705–15).

Sadūsī member of the clan of Sadūs, belonging to the large tribe of Shaybān, which had a substantial presence in the Jazīrah in the early Islamic period.

Saʿīd ibn ʿUqbah ibn Salm al-Hunāʾī (d. 167/784) son of a celebrated general; he held several minor governorships during the reigns of al-Manṣūr and al-Mahdī.

Ṣāliḥ ibn ʿAlī (d. 152/769) member of the Abbasid family who participated in the Abbasid revolution of 132/750 and held senior government positions in Egypt and Syria.

Sasanian (AD 224–652) pertaining to the House of Sasan, the dynasty from Fars in southwestern Iran that ruled the empire of Iran before it was conquered by the Muslims; admired as an example of wise and just government.

Sawād literally "blackness"; refers to the fertile black alluvial lands of southern Iraq where the Tigris and Euphrates rivers converge.

Shaqrān (d. ca. 19/640) Ethiopian Christian slave who was either given to or bought by the Prophet; he attended the latter's burial and transmitted sayings from him.

Shārī literally "seller"; a name used by Kharijites for themselves, usually explained as meaning a seller of one's life for God's cause.

Shaybān ibn Salamah (d. 130/748) a leader of the Kharijites in Khurasan, who initially allied with Abū Muslim against the Umayyad governor Naṣr ibn Sayyār but was himself killed by the Abbasid revolutionary forces.

Shuʿūbī one who adopts a cosmopolitan approach to culture, believing that the culture of all peoples (Ar. *shuʿūb*) is equally valid, and that "Arab" culture is not of greater significance than all others.

Sijistān the Arabic name of a province of southeastern Iran, known in Old Persian as Sakastan, "country of the Sakas," the latter being ancient Iranian nomads; al-Jāḥiẓ perhaps groups its residents with Bedouin Arabs as people of long memories since that was often regarded as a trait of nomads.

Sind the Indus valley region (from Sanskrit *sindhu*, meaning "river"), loosely corresponding to modern Pakistan.

Solomon (d. ca. 930) described in the Bible as the fourth king of the united monarchy of Israel and Judah and the builder of the first temple in Jerusalem; also honored in Christianity and Islam as a wise and pious ruler.

Ṣūfān people from several tribes who are said to have come together in the pre-Islamic period to serve at the Kaaba in Mecca and provide services for pilgrims.

Ṣufrī a member of the Kharijite subsect known as the Ṣufriyyah, based chiefly in northwestern Africa.

Tamīm large Arabian tribe, which chiefly inhabited the central and northern highlands of Najd in the pre-Islamic period before spreading across the Middle East in the wake of the Arab conquests.

Thamūd ancient western Arabian tribe mentioned in the Qur'an as a godless people who rejected the prophet Ṣāliḥ sent to them by God.

Thumāmah ibn Ashras (d. 213/828) rationalist theologian and administrative adviser who served at the court of the caliphs Hārūn al-Rashīd and al-Ma'mūn.

Ubullah ancient Apologos, at the mouth of the Tigris near Basra; al-Jāḥiẓ's reference to its fame for lithe dancers is not mentioned elsewhere, but it perhaps reflects its status as a port city with a diverse population from India and the Far East.

Uhbān ibn Aws a companion of Muḥammad who was informed by a wolf about the presence of a prophet in Medina.

ʿUkāshah ibn Miḥṣan (d. 12/633) a companion of the Prophet who participated in many of his military campaigns, including one led by him against the Banū Asad in the year 8/627.

Umayyads the first dynasty to rule the Islamic Empire, maintaining power for the period 40–132/661–750.

ʿUmar ibn al-Khaṭṭāb (r. 13–23/634–44) second of the rightly guided caliphs, who was a major force behind the early Muslim conquests and was revered for his humility and piety.

Usāmah ibn Zayd (d. ca. 54/674) a Mawla of the Prophet and a favorite of his, appointed by him just before his death to lead a campaign into southern Syria.

ʿUthmān (r. 23–35/644–56) son of ʿAffān, third of the rightly guided caliphs, who oversaw the conquest of the last provinces of the Sasanian Persian Empire.

al-Walīd ibn Ṭarīf (d. 180/796) Kharijite leader who launched a rebellion in the Jazīrah in 178/794, killed by Yazīd ibn Mazyad at the town of Hit on the Euphrates River.

al-Walīd (II) ibn Yazīd (r. 125–26/743–44), grandson of ʿĀtikah, wife of the Caliph ʿAbd al-Malik, and the eleventh Umayyad caliph; known for his generosity, but also for his love of poetry and wine drinking.

Yaḥyā ibn Muʿādh (d. 206/821) Khurasani general, active in the reign of al-Ma'mūn, who served as governor of the Jazīrah.

Yaʿlā ibn Munyah (d. 40s/660s) a member of the Balʿadawiyyah clan of the tribe of Tamīm and an ally of the Qurashī clan of Nawfal ibn ʿAbd Manāf; he was a Companion of the Prophet and served the caliphs ʿUmar and ʿUthmān in senior positions.

Yamāmī a resident of the central Arabian region of Yamāmah, which was a focus of Kharijite rebels opposed to the rule of the Prophet's tribe of Quraysh around the 70s/690s.

Yazīd ibn Mazyad (d. 183/799) famous Abbasid general who served under the caliphs al-Hādī and al-Rashīd as governor of Armenia and Azerbaijan.

Yazīd (III) ibn al-Walīd (r. 126/744) twelfth Umayyad caliph, nicknamed "the Deficient," allegedly because he cut military pay. He was the son of the Caliph al-Walīd I and his concubine Shāh-i Āfrīd, a Persian princess.

Yūlbā the Turk (fl. 180/796) name is uncertain (Harley Walker reads "Dūlabā"); fought a battle near Hit in Iraq with the Kharijite al-Walīd ibn Ṭarīf and killed him.

Zanjī member of an East African ethnic group living on or around the Swahili coast of modern Kenya and Tanzania; they served in large numbers, often as slaves, in the agricultural, commercial, and military sectors of the Islamic world.

Zayd ibn Ḥārithah (d. 8/629) sold as a slave in his teens and bought by an aunt of Khadījah, the first wife of the Prophet, who gifted him to the Prophet. The Prophet freed and adopted him, and he later entrusted him to lead military expeditions on his behalf.

Bibliography

Agha, Saleh Said. *The Revolution Which Toppled the Umayyads: Neither Arab nor ʿAbbāsid.* Brill, 2003.

———. "Language as a Component of Arab Identity in al-Jāḥiẓ: The Case of Ismāʿīl's Conversion to Arabhood." In *Al-Jāḥiẓ: A Muslim Humanist for Our Time*, edited by Arnim Heinemann, John Meloy, Tarif Khalidi, and Manfred Kropp. Orient-Institut Berlin, 2009.

Athamina, Khalil. "Non-Arab Regiments and Private Militias During the Umayyad Period." *Arabica* 45 (1998): 347–78.

Beeston, A. F. L. "Parallelism in Arabic Prose." *Journal of Arabic Literature* 5 (1974): 134–46.

———. *The Epistle on Singing-Girls by Jāḥiẓ*. Aris and Phillips, 1980.

———. "Review of: Nine Essays of al-Jahiz by W. M. Hutchins." *Journal of Arabic Literature* 20 (1989): 200–9.

Bennison, Amira K. *The Great Caliphs: The Golden Age of the Abbasid Empire*. I. B. Tauris, 2009.

Crone, Patricia. *Slaves on Horses: The Evolution of the Islamic Polity*. Cambridge University Press, 1981.

———. "The ʿAbbāsid Abnāʾ and Sāsānid Cavalrymen." *Journal of the Royal Asiatic Society* 3, no. 8 (1998): 1–19.

De la Vaissière, Étienne. *Samarcande et Samarra: Elites d'Asie Centrale dans l'Empire Abbasside*. Peeters, 2007.

El-Hibri, Tayeb. "Tabari's Biography of al-Muʿtasim: The Literary Use of a Military Career." *Der Islam* 86 (2011): 187–236.

Gabrieli, F. "La *risāla* di al-Ǧāḥiẓ sui Turchi." *Rivista degli Studi Orientali* 32 (1957): 477–83.

Gordon, Matthew. *The Breaking of a Thousand Swords: A History of the Turkish Military of Samarra (A.H. 200–275/815–889 C.E.)*. State University of New York Press, 2000.

———. "The Khāqānid Families of the Early Abbasid Period." *Journal of the American Oriental Society* 121 (2001): 236–55.

Gutas, Dimitri. *Greek Thought, Arabic Culture: The Graeco-Arabic Translation Movement in Baghdad and Early ʿAbbāsid Society (2nd–4th/5th–10th c.)*. Routledge, 1998.

Hagemann, Hannah-Lena. *The Kharijites in Early Islamic Historical Tradition: Heroes and Villains*. Edinburgh University Press, 2021.

Harley Walker, C. T. "Jahiz of Basra to Al-Fath ibn Khaqan on 'The Exploits of the Turks and the Army of the Khalifate in General.'" *Journal of the Royal Asiatic Society* (1915): 631–97.

Hefter, Thomas. *The Reader in al-Jāḥiẓ: The Epistolary Rhetoric of an Arabic Prose Master.* Edinburgh University Press, 2014.

Hutchins, William M. *Nine Essays of al-Jahiz.* Peter Lang, 1989.

Ibn Abī Shayba. *Al-Muṣannaf.* Edited by Kamāl Yūsuf al-Ḥūt. Maktabat al-ʿUlūm, 1989.

Ibn Ḥammād. *Kitāb al-Fitan.* Edited by Samīr Amīn al-Zuhayrī. Maktabat al-Tawḥīd, 1991.

Ibn Qutaybah. *The Excellence of the Arabs.* Edited and translated by James Montgomery, Peter Webb, and Sarah Bowen Savant. New York University Press, 2017.

Ibn Saʿd, Muḥammad. *Al-Ṭabaqāt al-kubrā.* Edited by Muḥammad ʿAbd al-Qādir ʿAṭā. Dār al-Kutub al-ʿIlmiyyah, 1990.

Al-Jāḥiẓ, ʿAmr ibn Baḥr. *Book of Misers.* Translated by R. B. Serjeant. Garnet Publishing, 1997.

———. *Al-Burṣān wa-l-ʿurjān wa-l-ʿumyān wa-l-ḥūlān.* Edited by ʿAbd al-Salām Hārūn. Dār al-Jīl, 1990.

———. "Fī manāqib al-Turk." In *Tria opuscula auctore Abu Othman ibn Bahr al-Djahiz Basrensi,* edited by Gerhof van Vloten. Brill, 1903.

———. "Fī manāqib al-Turk." In *Rasāʾil al-Jāḥiẓ,* vol. 1, edited by ʿAbd al-Salām Hārūn. Maktabat al-Khānjī, 1964.

———. "Fī manāqib al-Turk." In *Rasāʾil al-Jāḥiẓ,* vol. 3, edited by ʿAbd al-Salām Hārūn. Dār al-Jīl, 1991.

Kennedy, Hugh. *The Early Abbasid Caliphate: A Political History.* Croom Helm, 1981.

Lassner, Jacob. *The Shaping of Abbasid Rule.* Princeton University Press, 1980.

McDonald, M. V. "Al-Ǧāḥiẓ and His Analysis of the Turks." In *Law, Christianity and Modernism in Islamic Society: Proceedings of the Eighth Congress of the Union Européenne des Arabisants et Islamisants,* edited by U. Vermeulen and J. Van Reeth. Peters Press, 1998.

Montgomery, James E. *Al-Jāḥiẓ: In Praise of Books.* Edinburgh University Press, 2013.

Pellat, Charles. *Le milieu Baṣrien et la formation de Ǧāḥiẓ.* Adrien-Maisonneuve, 1953.

———. *The Life and Works of Jāḥiẓ: Translations of Selected Texts.* Translated by D. M. Hawke. University of California Press, 1969.

———. "Nouvel essai d'inventaire de l'oeuvre ǧāḥiẓienne." *Arabica* 31 (1984): 117–64.

Rescher, Oskar. "Das Schreiben des Dschâhiz an el-Fath ibn Khâqân, den Wezîr des khalifen el-Mutawakkil über 'Die Vorzüge der Türken.'" *Orientalistische Miszellen* (1925): 107–70.

Savran, Scott. Arabs and Iranians in the Islamic Conquest Narrative: Memory and Identity Construction in Islamic Historiography, 750–1050. Routledge, 2018.

Schoeler, Gregor. "Writing for a Reading Public: The Case of al-Jāḥiẓ." In *Al-Jāḥiẓ: A Muslim Humanist for Our Time*, edited by Arnim Heinemann, John Meloy, Tarif Khalidi, and Manfred Kropp. Orient-Institut Berlin, 2009.

Şeşen, Ramazan. "Cāḥiẓ'in eserlerinin Istanbul kütüphanelerindeki yazma nüshalari ve bunlar hakkinda bazi yeni malzameler." *Tarih Enstitüsü Dergisi* 1970: 231–72.

Al-Ṭabarī, Muḥammad ibn Jarīr. *Ta'rīkh al-rusul wa-l-mulūk*. Edited by M. J. de Goeje et al. Brill, 1879–1901.

Toorawa, Shawkat. *Ibn Abī Ṭāhir Ṭayfūr and Arabic Writerly Culture*. Routledge, 2010.

Turner, John P. "The *abnā' al-dawla*: The Definition and Legitimation of Identity in Response to the Fourth Fitna." *Journal of the American Oriental Society* 124 (2004): 1–22.

Urban, Elizabeth. *Conquered Populations in Early Islam: Non-Arabs, Slaves and the Sons of Slave Mothers*. Edinburgh University Press, 2020.

Van Ess, Josef. "Al-Jāḥiẓ and Early Muʿtazilī Theology." In *Al-Jāḥiẓ: A Muslim Humanist for Our Time*, edited by Arnim Heinemann, John Meloy, Tarif Khalidi, and Manfred Kropp. Orient-Institut Berlin, 2009.

Venuti, Lawrence. *The Translator's Invisibility: A History of Translation*. Revised edition. Routledge, 2008.

Vorhoeve, Petrus. *Handlist of Arabic Manuscripts in the Library of the University of Leiden and Other Collections in the Netherlands*. Bibliotheca Universitatis, 1957.

Webb, Peter. *Imagining the Arabs: Arab Identity and the Rise of Islam*. Edinburgh University Press, 2016.

Further Reading

Bakhtin, Mikhail. *The Dialogic Imagination: Four Essays*. Translated by Michael Holquist and Caryl Emerson. University of Texas Press, 1981.

Echiguer, Mohammed H. *Al-Ǧāḥiẓ et sa doctrine muʿtazilite*. Arabian Al Hilal, 1992.

Enderwitz, Susanne. *Gesellschaftlicher Rang und ethnische Legitimation: Der arabische Schriftsteller Abū ʿUṯmān al-Ǧāḥiẓ über die Afrikaner, Perser und Araber in der islamischen Gesellschaft*. Klaus Schwarz Verlag, 1979.

Hawting, Gerald. *The First Dynasty of Islam: The Umayyad Caliphate AD 661–750*. Second edition. Routledge, 2000.

Kennedy, Hugh. *The Armies of the Caliphs: Military and Society in the Early Islamic State*. Routledge, 2001.

———. *When Baghdad Ruled the Muslim World: The Rise and Fall of Islam's Greatest Dynasty*. Da Capo Press, 2005.

Kitapchi, Zekeriya. *Al-Turk fī muʾallifāt al-Jāḥiẓ wa-makānatuhum fī l-taʾrīkh al-islāmī* (*The Turks in the Works of al-Jahiz and Their Position in Islamic History*). Dār al-Thaqāfah, 1972.

Lee, Yonggyu. "Seeking Loyalty: The Inner Asian Tradition of Personal Guards and Its Influence in Persia and China." PhD diss., Harvard University, 2004.

Northedge, Alastair. *The Historical Topography of Samarra*. The British School of Archeology in Iraq, 2005.

Al-Qadi, Wadad. "Dislocation and Nostalgia: Al-ḥanīn ilā al-awṭān; Expressions of Alienation in Early Arabic Literature." In *Myths, Historical Archetypes and Symbolic Figures in Arabic Literature: Towards a New Hermeneutic Approach*, edited by Angelika Neuwirth, Birgit Embaló, Sebastian Günther, and Maher Jarrar. Steiner, 1999.

Van Ess, Josef. *Theology and Society in the Second and Third Centuries of the Hijra: A History of Religious Thought in Early Islam*. Brill, 2016–20.

Index of Arabic Poetry

Section	Poet	Lines	Meter	Rhyme
		ب		
§7.23	unidentified poet	1	*ṭawīl*	عَجِبْ
§4.15	unidentified poet	1	*ṭawīl*	ٱلْمُهَذَّبُ
		ت		
§4.19	Muḥammad ibn Saʿīd	3	*ṭawīl*	جَلَّتِ
		ر		
§7.23	unidentified poet	2	*ṭawīl*	ٱلْبَرَابِرِ
§8.12	unidentified poet	2	*ṭawīl*	مُهْرِ
§7.27	Aws ibn Ḥajar	1	*basīṭ*	بَيَازِيرُ
		ف		
§7.19	Aws ibn Ḥajar	1	*ṭawīl*	وَرَاصِفُ
§5.6	unidentified poet	1	*ṭawīl*	ٱلْمُجَفَّفِ
		ل		
§7.27	Khalaf al-Aḥmar	1	*wāfir*	ٱلسِّبَالِ
§6.7	unidentified poet	1	*wāfir*	زَوَالِ
§5.22	unidentified poet	1	*kāmil*	وَمُنَازِلُ
§5.22	al-Ḍabbī	1	*kāmil*	أَنْزِلِ
§7.26	ʿAmallas ibn ʿAqīl ibn ʿUllafah	1	*ṭawīl*	حِسْلِ
§5.22	unidentified poet	1	*khafīf*	ٱلنُّزُولَا
§5.6	unidentified poet	1	*wāfir*	بِٱلْأَصِيلِ
		ن		
§8.11	unidentified poet	1	*rajaz*	مَرْوَانْ

Section	Poet	Lines	Meter	Rhyme
		ه		
§4.17	Bashshār	3	*ṭawīl*	تُعَاتِبُهْ
§4.16	Ḥarīsh al-Saʿdī	2	*ṭawīl*	خُطُوبُهَا
§4.18	Muṭīʿ ibn Iyās al-Laythī	3	*khafīf*	نَعْلُهْ
		ي		
§5.6	unidentified poet	1	*sarīʿ*	ٱلشَّارِي

Index

About the NYUAD Research Institute

The Library of Arabic Literature is a research center affiliated with NYU Abu Dhabi and is supported by a grant from the NYU Abu Dhabi Research Institute.

The NYU Abu Dhabi Research Institute is a world-class center of cutting-edge and innovative research, scholarship, and cultural activity. It supports centers that address questions of global significance and local relevance and allows leading faculty members from across the disciplines to carry out creative scholarship and high-level research on a range of complex issues with depth, scale, and longevity that otherwise would not be possible.

From genomics and climate science to the humanities and Arabic literature, Research Institute centers make significant contributions to scholarship, scientific understanding, and artistic creativity. Centers strengthen cross-disciplinary engagement and innovation among the faculty, build critical mass in infrastructure and research talent at NYU Abu Dhabi, and have helped make the university a magnet for outstanding faculty, scholars, students, and international collaborations.

About the Typefaces

The Arabic text is set in Sakkal Kitab Medium, a font from the Sakkal Kitab family of fonts designed by Mamoun Sakkal and Aida Sakkal. Sakkal Kitab is an Arabic Naskh text typeface family with elegant cursive tatweel/kashida and swashes in multiple lengths. It is ideal for setting long text passages in books and magazines. The family has five well coordinated weights.

The English text is set in Adobe Text, a new and versatile text typeface family designed by Robert Slimbach for Western (Latin, Greek, Cyrillic) typesetting. Its workhorse qualities make it perfect for a wide variety of applications, especially for longer passages of text where legibility and economy are important. Adobe Text bridges the gap between calligraphic Renaissance types of the fifteenth and sixteenth centuries and high-contrast Modern styles of the 18th century, taking many of its design cues from early post-Renaissance Baroque transitional types cut by designers such as Christoffel van Dijck, Nicolaus Kis, and William Caslon. While grounded in classical form, Adobe Text is also a statement of contemporary utilitarian design, well suited to a wide variety of print and on-screen applications.

Titles Published by the Library of Arabic Literature

For more details on individual titles, visit www.libraryofarabicliterature.org

Classical Arabic Literature: A Library of Arabic Literature Anthology
Selected and translated by Geert Jan van Gelder (2012)

A Treasury of Virtues: Sayings, Sermons, and Teachings of ʿAlī, by al-Qāḍī al-Quḍāʿī, with the **One Hundred Proverbs** attributed to al-Jāḥiẓ
Edited and translated by Tahera Qutbuddin (2013)

The Epistle on Legal Theory, by al-Shāfiʿī
Edited and translated by Joseph E. Lowry (2013)

Leg over Leg, by Aḥmad Fāris al-Shidyāq
Edited and translated by Humphrey Davies (4 volumes; 2013–14)

Virtues of the Imām Aḥmad ibn Ḥanbal, by Ibn al-Jawzī
Edited and translated by Michael Cooperson (2 volumes; 2013–15)

The Epistle of Forgiveness, by Abū l-ʿAlāʾ al-Maʿarrī
Edited and translated by Geert Jan van Gelder and Gregor Schoeler (2 volumes; 2013–14)

The Principles of Sufism, by ʿĀʾishah al-Bāʿūniyyah
Edited and translated by Th. Emil Homerin (2014)

The Expeditions: An Early Biography of Muḥammad, by Maʿmar ibn Rāshid
Edited and translated by Sean W. Anthony (2014)

Two Arabic Travel Books

Accounts of China and India, by Abū Zayd al-Sīrāfī
Edited and translated by Tim Mackintosh-Smith (2014)

Mission to the Volga, by Aḥmad ibn Faḍlān
Edited and translated by James Montgomery (2014)

Disagreements of the Jurists: A Manual of Islamic Legal Theory, by al-Qāḍī al-Nuʿmān
Edited and translated by Devin J. Stewart (2015)

Consorts of the Caliphs: Women and the Court of Baghdad, by Ibn al-Sāʿī
Edited by Shawkat M. Toorawa and translated by the Editors of the Library of Arabic Literature (2015)

What ʿĪsā ibn Hishām Told Us, by Muḥammad al-Muwayliḥī
Edited and translated by Roger Allen (2 volumes; 2015)

The Life and Times of Abū Tammām, by Abū Bakr Muḥammad ibn Yaḥyā al-Ṣūlī
Edited and translated by Beatrice Gruendler (2015)

The Sword of Ambition: Bureaucratic Rivalry in Medieval Egypt, by ʿUthmān ibn Ibrāhīm al-Nābulusī
Edited and translated by Luke Yarbrough (2016)

Brains Confounded by the Ode of Abū Shādūf Expounded, by Yūsuf al-Shirbīnī
Edited and translated by Humphrey Davies (2 volumes; 2016)

Light in the Heavens: Sayings of the Prophet Muḥammad, by al-Qāḍī al-Quḍāʿī
Edited and translated by Tahera Qutbuddin (2016)

Risible Rhymes, by Muḥammad ibn Maḥfūẓ al-Sanhūrī
Edited and translated by Humphrey Davies (2016)

A Hundred and One Nights
Edited and translated by Bruce Fudge (2016)

The Excellence of the Arabs, by Ibn Qutaybah
Edited by James E. Montgomery and Peter Webb
Translated by Sarah Bowen Savant and Peter Webb (2017)

Scents and Flavors: A Syrian Cookbook
Edited and translated by Charles Perry (2017)

Arabian Satire: Poetry from 18th-Century Najd, by Ḥmēdān al-Shwēʿir
Edited and translated by Marcel Kurpershoek (2017)

In Darfur: An Account of the Sultanate and Its People, by Muḥammad ibn ʿUmar al-Tūnisī
Edited and translated by Humphrey Davies (2 volumes; 2018)

War Songs, by ʿAntarah ibn Shaddād
Edited by James E. Montgomery
Translated by James E. Montgomery with Richard Sieburth (2018)

Arabian Romantic: Poems on Bedouin Life and Love, by ʿAbdallāh ibn Sbayyil
Edited and translated by Marcel Kurpershoek (2018)

Dīwān ʿAntarah ibn Shaddād: A Literary-Historical Study
By James E. Montgomery (2018)

Stories of Piety and Prayer: Deliverance Follows Adversity, by al-Muḥassin ibn ʿAlī al-Tanūkhī
Edited and translated by Julia Bray (2019)

The Philosopher Responds: An Intellectual Correspondence from the Tenth Century, by Abū Ḥayyān al-Tawḥīdī and Abū ʿAlī Miskawayh
Edited by Bilal Orfali and Maurice A. Pomerantz
Translated by Sophia Vasalou and James E. Montgomery (2 volumes; 2019)

Tajrīd sayf al-himmah li-stikhrāj mā fī dhimmat al-dhimmah: A Scholarly Edition of ʿUthmān ibn Ibrāhīm al-Nābulusī's Text
By Luke Yarbrough (2020)

The Discourses: Reflections on History, Sufism, Theology, and Literature—Volume One, by al-Ḥasan al-Yūsī
Edited and translated by Justin Stearns (2020)

Impostures, by al-Ḥarīrī
Translated by Michael Cooperson (2020)

Maqāmāt Abī Zayd al-Sarūjī, by al-Ḥarīrī
Edited by Michael Cooperson (2020)

The Yoga Sutras of Patañjali, by Abū Rayḥān al-Bīrūnī
Edited and translated by Mario Kozah (2020)

The Book of Charlatans, by Jamāl al-Dīn ʿAbd al-Raḥīm al-Jawbarī
Edited by Manuela Dengler
Translated by Humphrey Davies (2020)

A Physician on the Nile: A Description of Egypt and Journal of the Famine Years, by ʿAbd al-Laṭīf al-Baghdādī
Edited and translated by Tim Mackintosh-Smith (2021)

The Book of Travels, by Ḥannā Diyāb
Edited by Johannes Stephan
Translated by Elias Muhanna (2 volumes; 2021)

Kalīlah and Dimnah: Fables of Virtue and Vice, by Ibn al-Muqaffaʿ
Edited by Michael Fishbein
Translated by Michael Fishbein and James E. Montgomery (2021)

Love, Death, Fame: Poetry and Lore from the Emirati Oral Tradition, by al-Māyidī ibn Ẓāhir
Edited and translated by Marcel Kurpershoek (2022)

The Essence of Reality: A Defense of Philosophical Sufism, by ʿAyn al-Quḍāt
Edited and translated by Mohammed Rustom (2022)

The Requirements of the Sufi Path: A Defense of the Mystical Tradition, by Ibn Khaldūn
Edited and translated by Carolyn Baugh (2022)

The Doctors' Dinner Party, by Ibn Buṭlān
Edited and translated by Philip F. Kennedy and Jeremy Farrell (2023)

Fate the Hunter: Early Arabic Hunting Poems
Edited and translated by James E. Montgomery (2023)

The Book of Monasteries, by al-Shābushtī
Edited and translated by Hilary Kilpatrick (2023)

In Deadly Embrace: Arabic Hunting Poems, by Ibn al-Muʿtazz
Edited and translated by James E. Montgomery (2023)

The Divine Names: A Mystical Theology of the Names of God in the Qur'an, by ʿAfīf al-Dīn al-Tilimsānī
Edited and translated by Yousef Casewit (2023)

Bedouin Poets of the Nafūd Desert, by Khalaf Abū Zwayyid, ʿAdwān al-Hirbīd, and ʿAjlān ibn Rmāl
Edited and translated by Marcel Kurpershoek (2024)

The Rules of Logic, by Najm al-Dīn al-Kātibī
Edited and translated by Tony Street **(2024)**

Najm al-Dīn al-Kātibī's Al-Risālah al-Shamsiyyah: An Edition and Translation with Commentary
By Tony Street **(2024)**

Arabian Hero: Oral Poetry and Narrative Lore from Northern Arabia, by Shāyiʿ al-Amsaḥ
Edited and translated by Marcel Kurpershoek **(2024)**

A Demon Spirit: Arabic Hunting Poems, by Abū Nuwās
Edited and translated by James E. Montgomery **(2024)**

The Genius of Invective: Ibn Zaydūn's Letter Explained, by Ibn Nubātah
Edited and translated by Peter Webb **(2025)**

The Turks and the Caliphal Army, by al-Jāḥiẓ
Edited and translated by Robert G. Hoyland **(2025)**

English-only Paperbacks

Leg over Leg, by Aḥmad Fāris al-Shidyāq **(2 volumes; 2015)**
The Expeditions: An Early Biography of Muḥammad, by Maʿmar ibn Rāshid **(2015)**
The Epistle on Legal Theory: A Translation of al-Shāfiʿī's *Risālah*, by al-Shāfiʿī **(2015)**
The Epistle of Forgiveness, by Abū l-ʿAlāʾ al-Maʿarrī **(2016)**
The Principles of Sufism, by ʿĀʾishah al-Bāʿūniyyah **(2016)**
A Treasury of Virtues: Sayings, Sermons, and Teachings of ʿAlī, by al-Qāḍī al-Quḍāʿī, with the **One Hundred Proverbs** attributed to al-Jāḥiẓ **(2016)**
The Life of Ibn Ḥanbal, by Ibn al-Jawzī **(2016)**
Mission to the Volga, by Ibn Faḍlān **(2017)**
Accounts of China and India, by Abū Zayd al-Sīrāfī **(2017)**
A Hundred and One Nights (2017)
Consorts of the Caliphs: Women and the Court of Baghdad, by Ibn al-Sāʿī **(2017)**
Disagreements of the Jurists: A Manual of Islamic Legal Theory, by al-Qāḍī al-Nuʿmān **(2017)**

What ʿĪsā ibn Hishām Told Us, by Muḥammad al-Muwayliḥī (2018)
War Songs, by ʿAntarah ibn Shaddād (2018)
The Life and Times of Abū Tammām, by Abū Bakr Muḥammad ibn Yaḥyā al-Ṣūlī (2018)
The Sword of Ambition, by ʿUthmān ibn Ibrāhīm al-Nābulusī (2019)
Brains Confounded by the Ode of Abū Shādūf Expounded: Volume One, by Yūsuf al-Shirbīnī (2019)
Brains Confounded by the Ode of Abū Shādūf Expounded: Volume Two, by Yūsuf al-Shirbīnī and **Risible Rhymes**, by Muḥammad ibn Maḥfūẓ al-Sanhūrī (2019)
The Excellence of the Arabs, by Ibn Qutaybah (2019)
Light in the Heavens: Sayings of the Prophet Muḥammad, by al-Qāḍī al-Quḍāʿī (2019)
Scents and Flavors: A Syrian Cookbook (2020)
Arabian Satire: Poetry from 18th-Century Najd, by Ḥmēdān al-Shwēʿir (2020)
In Darfur: An Account of the Sultanate and Its People, by Muḥammad al-Tūnisī (2020)
Arabian Romantic: Poems on Bedouin Life and Love, by ʿAbdallāh ibn Sbayyil (2020)
The Philosopher Responds, by Abū Ḥayyān al-Tawḥīdī and Abū ʿAlī Miskawayh (2021)
Impostures, by al-Ḥarīrī (2021)
The Discourses: Reflections on History, Sufism, Theology, and Literature—Volume One, by al-Ḥasan al-Yūsī (2021)
The Book of Charlatans, by Jamāl al-Dīn ʿAbd al-Raḥīm al-Jawbarī (2022)
The Yoga Sutras of Patañjali, by Abū Rayḥān al-Bīrūnī (2022)
The Book of Travels, by Ḥannā Diyāb (2022)
A Physician on the Nile: A Description of Egypt and Journal of the Famine Years, by ʿAbd al-Laṭīf al-Baghdādī (2022)
Kalīlah and Dimnah: Fables of Virtue and Vice, by Ibn al-Muqaffaʿ (2023)
Love, Death, Fame: Poetry and Lore from the Emirati Oral Tradition, by al-Māyidī ibn Ẓāhir (2023)
The Essence of Reality: A Defense of Philosophical Sufism, by ʿAyn al-Quḍāt (2023)
The Doctors' Dinner Party, by Ibn Buṭlān (2024)
The Requirements of the Sufi Path: A Defense of the Mystical Tradition, by Ibn Khaldūn (2024)

Fate the Hunter: Early Arabic Hunting Poems (2024)
The Book of Monasteries, by al-Shābushtī (2025)
In Deadly Embrace: Arabic Hunting Poems, by Ibn al-Muʿtazz (2025)
The Divine Names: A Mystical Theology of the Names of God in the Qurʾan, by ʿAfīf al-Dīn al-Tilimsānī (2025)
Bedouin Poets of the Nafūd Desert, by Khalaf Abū Zwayyid, ʿAdwān al-Hirbīd, and ʿAjlān ibn Rmāl (2025)
The Rules of Logic, by Najm al-Dīn al-Kātibī (2025)

About the Editor–Translator

Robert G. Hoyland is a Professor of Late Antique and Early Islamic Middle Eastern History at New York University. He is the author of *Seeing Islam as Others Saw It* (1997), *Arabia and the Arabs* (2001), and *In God's Path: The Arab Conquests and the Creation of an Islamic Empire* (2014).

www.ingramcontent.com/pod-product-compliance
Lightning Source LLC
Chambersburg PA
CBHW030533310726
48979CB00010B/1896/J

* 9 7 8 1 4 7 9 8 4 0 6 2 5 *